Weddings

(Originally: *Planning the Perfect Wedding*)

Emily Post Series

Weddings

(Originally: *Planning the Perfect Wedding*)

What every bride should know about wedding etiquette and arrangements for the formal and informal wedding.

BY ROSALIE BRODY

A Fireside Book
Published by Simon and Schuster in association with the Emily Post Institute, Inc.

Emily Post Institute
Advisory Board

Copyright © 1963 by Emily Post Institute, Inc.
as *Planning the Perfect Wedding*
All rights reserved
including the right of reproduction
in whole or in part in any form
A Fireside Book
Published by Simon and Schuster
A Division of Gulf & Western Corporation
Simon & Schuster Building
Rockefeller Center, 1230 Avenue of the Americas
New York, New York 10020
FIRESIDE and colophon are registered
trademarks of Simon & Schuster, Inc.
ISBN 0-671-22048-9
Library of Congress Catalog Card Number 63-9158
Designed by Bevans, Marks & Barrow, Inc.
Manufactured in the United States of America
23 Pbk.

Contents

●

Contents continued

Preface

Emily Post has long been considered the reigning authority on wedding etiquette and gracious living. Excellence and perfection have been her ideals. Today her name has become a hallmark in America for the ultimate in good taste, courtesy, and charm. All of these attributes are revealed most exquisitely in the perfect wedding.

Emily Post might well have compared a wedding to a poem, for deep inside of each are thoughts and sentiments that last a lifetime. And if, as Robert Frost has said, "a poem should begin in delight and end in wisdom," so the perfect wedding should begin in graciousness and end in beauty. The pattern is flexible, the ingredients are of your choice. Only the meaningful, important rules of etiquette remain unchangeable.

To help you achieve a perfect wedding, the Emily Post Institute offers you this modern guide.* Here you will find a valuable key to engagement and wedding etiquette, as well as practical pointers on wedding arrangements, invitations and announcements, showers and parties, bridal attire, floral decorations, gifts, re-

---

* For rules of etiquette on military or clergyman's weddings, consult Emily Post's *Etiquette, The Blue Book of Social Usage* (New York: Funk & Wagnalls Co., 1960).

Preface continued

freshments for the reception, and more. Let this book be your incentive to choose the kind of wedding you really want and to make it come true.

As a final word, your wedding should reflect the dignity and beauty of this great occasion, infused with tradition and your own imagination.

Ever since her first children's party, Rosalie Brody, a professional writer who lives in Manhattan, has been interested in party-giving and party-going, including wedding receptions big and small. In all her party planning, Mrs. Brody follows Emily Post's common-sense ap-proach: weddings and wedding parties are simpler, easier, and more enjoyable if the right thing is done the right way at the right time. In this book she shows prospective brides how to plan a wed-ding and reception that not only suits the individual and her budget but also con-siders the comfort and pleasure of the wedding guest. Mrs. Brody has put her theories about social usage to work in research as a "woman's angle" consult-ant and as an advisor on home services.

E. P. I.

Introduction

Several years ago I was asked to revise and modernize Emily Post's *Etiquette*. Although it had been revised in ten previous editions since its original appearance in 1922, no major changes had been made since Emily Post's death in 1960. As her granddaughter-in-law, I was chosen to take on the job, and so began a most fascinating, surprising, and satisfying experience.

Most of us take acceptable behavior for granted, and do not consider the reasons behind the seemingly natural courtesy which is a part of our everyday life.

Although the concept of manners and accepted behavior changes constantly, the basis for all etiquette *never* changes. It is, after all, a code of behavior, a way of life based on kindness, consideration, and self-respect. Etiquette rules, and the books defining them, are merely guidelines to help one live according to that code.

In spite of the many changes in our way of life, the etiquette of weddings remains basically unchanged. This is the one moment in every girl's life which must be absolutely perfect. It is also the time when most girls, no matter how independent and self-reliant, return to tradition. At one time I thought that weddings tended to be less formal than

Introduction *continued*

they were years ago. Through the readers of my newspaper column, "Doing the Right Thing," and the thousands of girls I talk to personally, I find that more than ever before they are planning large, elaborate weddings. Naturally, this occasion brings with it many problems and questions. A bride, and a mother who is planning a wedding for her daughter, must turn to someone for help. Emily Post's *Weddings* solves every conceivable problem in the most complete and concise manner.

As one who has answered so many queries about every phase of marriage, I can truthfully say that this book will be an invaluable aid to the prospective bride in planning her perfect wedding.

Elizabeth L. Post

Weddings

Announcing the Engagement

So you have said "Yes" to the man of your choice, and you are engaged! All best wishes for your happiness. May this be a joyous prelude to a perfect wedding and a long and happy life together.

The first step in the dignified procedure of wedding etiquette is announcing the engagement. Once consent has been given and both families have met, the formal or public announcement is made by the parents of the bride-to-be. The private announcement, usually made at a party for intimate friends, precedes the newspaper announcement.

The Engagement Party

The engagement party may take the form of a luncheon, tea, cocktail party, or "at home" reception. At this time, the bride-to-be or her mother breaks the news to friends as they arrive and are introduced to the fiancé. At a dinner party, the news is often announced by the father who rises and proposes a toast to the health of his daughter and future son-in-law.

Invitations to the engagement party, or dinner, are extended by the mother-of-the-bride by telephone or personal notes. On her own engraved "informals" or on plain note paper, she writes the details of the party in this fashion:

Cocktails
at the Jones'
Saturday, March 24, 5 to 7

R.s.v.p.   *100 Park Avenue*
NU 8-3234   *New York*

Emily Post's Points of Propriety

Engraved or printed engagement announcements are *not* correct.

No mention of the engagement appears on the invitation.

Before an engagement is announced publicly, the groom asks the consent of the bride's father (or head of her family) and the groom's family calls on the bride's family where it is at all possible.

An engagement is announced three to four months before the wedding, and never more than a year ahead.

ENGAGEMENT LUNCHEON
Veal Shower Salad
Cheese and Pimiento Circles
Peach Blush Tarts
Coffee

Veal Shower Salad

1½ cups veal
6 cups water
1 small carrot
2 celery tops
2 slices onion
4 peppercorns
3 whole cloves
1½ teaspoons salt
3 envelopes unflavored gelatin
1 tablespoon lemon juice
1 teaspoon salt
Pimiento-stuffed green olives, sliced
½ cup real mayonnaise
¾ cup chopped celery
3 hard cooked eggs, chopped
Salad greens

Combine veal, water, carrot, celery tops, onion, peppercorns, cloves, and 1½ teaspoons salt in kettle. Bring to boil, then reduce heat and simmer until veal is tender, 1½ to 2 hours. Remove meat and chop fine. Strain stock; cool and skim off fat. Measure 5½ cups stock.

Sprinkle 2½ envelopes gelatin on 1 cup stock to soften. Bring 4 cups stock to boil, remove from heat. Add softened gelatin and stir until completely dissolved. Mix in lemon juice and 1 teaspoon salt. Spoon 2 tablespoons mixture into bottom of 2-quart mold; allow to set, then arrange olive slices in desired pattern on top. Chill remaining gelatin-stock mixture until it reaches the consistency of unbeaten egg white.

Meanwhile, combine remaining ½ cup stock and ½ envelope gelatin in saucepan. Heat slowly, stirring constantly, until gelatin is completely dissolved. Gradually mix into mayonnaise. Chill until mixture begins to thicken, then spoon over olive slices in mold. Chill until almost firm.

When gelatin-stock mixture reaches egg white consistency, mix in chopped veal, celery, and eggs. Spoon carefully over mayonnaise mixture in mold. Chill until firm. Unmold on serving plate. Garnish with salad greens and, if desired, serve with additional mayonnaise. Makes 12 servings.

Cheese and Pimiento Circles

24 slices white bread
2 cups firmly packed grated Cheddar
cheese
1/3 cup real mayonnaise
Worcestershire sauce
Pimiento strips

Cut each bread slice with cutters to make
1 (2½-inch) and 1 (1½-inch) circle. Blend
cheese, mayonnaise, and Worcestershire
sauce. Spread on large bread circles. Top
with small circles. Garnish with pimiento
strips. Makes 24.

Peach Blush Tarts

TART SHELLS:

2 cups sifted flour
½ teaspoon salt
½ cup corn oil or balanced oil margarine
¼ cup creamy or chunk style peanut
butter
5 tablespoons cold water

FILLING:

1 (8-ounce) jar red currant jelly
2 (1 pound 13-ounce) cans sliced
peaches, drained
Whipped cream

Mix flour and salt together; place 1 cup in
mixing bowl. Cut in margarine and peanut
butter with pastry blender or 2 knives until
coarse crumbs form, then cut in remaining
flour mixture. Sprinkle with 1 tablespoon
water; toss with fork until mixed. Repeat
with remaining water, 1 tablespoon at a
time. Gather dough into ball; divide into
thirds. Roll out each third on lightly floured
board to very thin circle. Cut into 5-inch
rounds. Press each into tart pan or over
bottom of custard cup. Prick with fork.
Bake in 400°F. (hot) oven until lightly
browned, about 10 minutes. Cool in pan.

Melt jelly in saucepan over medium heat,
stirring constantly. Chill until thickened,
about 1 hour. Arrange peach slices in tart
shells; top with currant jelly sauce. Garnish
with whipped cream. Makes about 12 peach
tarts.

The Newspaper Announcement

Public announcement is made by noti-
fying the society editor of the daily
papers that Mr. and Mrs. John Jones of
100 Park Avenue announce the engagement of their daughter, Mildred, to Mr.
George Brown, son of Mr. and Mrs.
Emerson Brown of New Orleans. Mention of the couple's schools, military
service, company or business association,
clubs, and grandparents may also be included, as well as a photograph of the
bride.

When a girl's parents are not living,
her engagement is announced by her
nearest relative: grandparent, aunt, or
older sister. Otherwise, she may word
the announcement as follows: "The engagement of Miss Mary Smith, daughter
of the late Mr. and Mrs. Samuel Smith,
is announced to Mr. Henry Brown," etc.

When parents are divorced, the engagement should be announced by the
girl's mother, unless she lives with her
father. However, the other parents' name
should be mentioned in the notice. Or
both names may be given to the newspapers impersonally this way: "The
engagement of Miss Mary Robinson,
daughter of Mr. Stephen Robinson and
Mrs. Smith Robinson (or Mrs. John
Jones, if her mother is married again),
is announced to Mr. Henry Brown, son
of," etc.

When a woman of forty or more be-
comes engaged, she and her fiancé usually tell their friends and relatives shortly
before the wedding. A widow announces

her second engagement the same way, although both may give the announcements to the society editors of the papers. Traditionally, no formal announcement is made of a divorcée's engagement.

The Engagement Ring

The engagement ring is worn for the first time in public on the day of the announcement. An engagement ring, however, is not essential to the validity of the betrothal. Countless wives have never had engagement rings, others have received rings long after their marriage, and many brides prefer to forego a ring for more practical investments in home and household. Nevertheless, the engagement ring remains a charming and elegant gift.

A sparkling variety of stones and settings are appropriate from the diamond solitaire or heirloom ring to a semi-precious gem or birthstone ring. The choice, however, should be made by the bride-to-be. She should be asked to help choose the stone and the setting, or at least to choose from a small selection put aside in advance by her fiancé.

An engagement present for the man —while unnecessary—is not improper. Studs, cuff links, watch bands, watches, cigarette cases, and key chains are popular gifts, and a ring, though rarely given, is acceptable.

Choosing the Wedding Ring or Rings

It is both customary and important for the bride to choose her wedding band. The plain band of gold is still in finest taste, although many brides prefer a more elaborate one.

If the bridegroom wishes to wear a wedding band, the bride buys his gold band in any style he prefers. Matching bands have become increasingly popular. Both rings may be engraved with appropriate sentiments, but the width usually restricts the quotation to the initials of the couple and the date of the wedding: *A.Y.X. and L.M.N. September 2, 1963.*

The Broken Engagement

In the case of a broken engagement the engagement ring and other gifts must be returned. A notice reading "The engagement of Miss Sara Black and Mr. John Doe has been broken by mutual consent" is sent to the newspapers which announced the engagement.

2

Plans and Pointers for a Perfect Wedding

While a large, fashionable wedding can amount to several thousand dollars, plans vary and the largest expenses are the most elastic. Whatever size or style of wedding you choose, it is the *careful, thoughtful planning*—not the cost—that makes it beautiful. It is never how much you spend but how well you spend it that matters. And the simplest affair is often the most elegant.

Tradition says that the bride's parents pay all wedding expenses, although many of today's brides assume a major share of the financial responsibility.

EXPENSES OF THE BRIDE'S PARENTS INCLUDE:

Engraved invitations and announcements.*

The bridal gown, headdress, accessories and trousseau.

Bouquets, corsages, and floral decorations.

Music for the wedding.

Bridal photographs and candid pictures.

Transportation (rented cars or limousines).

Champagne, wedding cake, and all other items of the reception.

The bride's presents to her bridesmaids, and their hotel accommodations if necessary.

A wedding present to the bride in addition to her trousseau.

The bridegroom's ring or wedding present—or both—if the bride wishes to give them.

Rental of church awnings and aisle canvas. (Correct for all large, formal church or home weddings in the city; required in the country for bad weather only.)

THE BRIDEGROOM'S EXPENSES TRADITIONALLY INCLUDE:

The engagement and wedding rings.

A wedding present to the bride (fine jewelry or something for her personal adornment).

A personal gift to his best man and ushers, and their hotel expenses.

Wedding ties, gloves, and boutonnières for ushers, plus his own boutonnière.

His bachelor dinner (if he gives one).

The bride's bouquet (where local custom requires it) and the bride's going-away corsage (unless this is taken from her bridal bouquet).

The clergyman's fee.

The marriage license.

Transportation for himself and his best man to the ceremony.

All expenses of the wedding trip.

* While true engraving is a required expense for an ultra-formal, ultra-perfect wedding, a new method of simulating engraving is entirely acceptable where cost must be considered.

"Dollars-and-Sense" Planning

An over-all budget, based on what you and your parents can afford, will spare you the nightmare of unsolved financial problems and unnecessary debts. For a realistic picture of the actual expenses of four different weddings, consult the wedding expense chart below. Remember, these figures are offered only as examples to help you coordinate your own plans most efficiently.

A Guide to Wedding Costs

Total Wedding Budget	$500		$1,000		$1,500		$4,000	
ITEMS TO BUDGET								
Wedding Clothes	$125	25%	$200	20%	$300	20%	$680	17%
Invitations, Announcements, etc.	25	5%	40	4%	60	4%	200	5%
Flowers, Attendants at Church and Reception	50	10%	80	8%	120	8%	400	10%
Music (Church and Reception)	35	7%	40	4%	120	8%	400	10%
Transportation for Bridal Party to Church and Reception	none		40	4%	75	5%	160	4%
Photographs—Formal and Candids	50	10%	100	10%	150	10%	240	6%
Bridesmaids' Gifts	25	5%	40	4%	60	4%	120	3%
Bridal Party Entertainment at Rehearsal (optional)	10	2%	30	3%	45	3%	200	5%
Reception (Food, Beverages, Wedding Cake, Catering Service)	175	35%	400	40%	525	35%	1,400	35%
Contingency Fund (Any additional expenses not planned in original budget.)	5	1%	30	3%	45	3%	200	5%

The $500 wedding: Informal or formal with one or two attendants; a reception for fifty held at home or in church facilities.

The $1,000 wedding: Formal with two to four attendants and a reception for one hundred.

The $1,500 wedding: Formal with two to four attendants with buffet reception for one hundred to one hundred fifty at club or hotel.

The $4,000 wedding: Formal with six to eight attendants and reception for one hundred to three hundred at club or hotel (either buffet or sit-down depending on number).

The Bride's Checklist

Your wedding will be as correct as it is lovely if you follow the pattern given below. Worthy of special note are the pertinent points of propriety and graciousness that dignify each detail, and make each event a joy for everyone.

To use this chapter most productively, read it over quickly for a general overview of what is involved. Then go back, with pencil and calendar in hand, and start your own checklist.

Arrangements for a large, formal wedding take at least three months. So, the sooner you begin, the more time you will have later on for writing "thank you" notes, partying, and getting your "beauty rest."

Three Months Ahead of the Wedding

1. *Decide what type of wedding you will have,* whether it will be formal, semi-formal, or informal, and if it will be held at a church, club, hotel, or home. Your bridal gown, the number of attendants you will have, and the hour of the ceremony determine the degree of formality; so be sure to consult your groom and your family whose expenses will be affected by the type of wedding you choose.

2. *Decide the hour of the ceremony and the type of reception to follow.* Remember, the degree of formality in your wedding ceremony should be matched in your reception. A formal high-noon church ceremony is usually followed by a complete luncheon menu, a late afternoon wedding by a reception supper, and a mid-afternoon ceremony by a tea or cocktail reception.

   Religion, climate, custom, and transportation schedules for guests may also be important factors, as well as plans for your own wedding trip. In the South and throughout the West, the smartest weddings take place in the evening (usually between eight and nine P.M.) when the heat of the day has passed, and guests wear evening clothes.

3. *Decide the date of the wedding.* Find out when your clergyman is free to perform the ceremony, and when the church or chapel is available. You will probably want to visit your clergyman with your fiancé to discuss personal matters as well as wedding details. At this time, you should also inquire about any restrictions as to time of year, day of week, musical selections, floral

decorations, or style of wedding clothes. You might also check with him on the rental fee for the church, organist's fee, whether the church chimes may be used, if a candlelight service is permissible, if the social hall is available that day for a reception, if arrangements for a policeman or parking attendant may be made through the church secretary.

Before confirming the church date, be sure that the club, caterer, or hotel selected for your reception can accommodate you and your party at the proper time. For details on reception plans, see pages 81–98.

4. *Decide on how many guests and attendants you will have.* For a large church wedding, a bride may have as many as ten bridesmaids—flower girls, pages, train bearers, and a ring bearer. But regardless of the size of the wedding, she should have at least one attendant—her maid or matron of honor. The groom always has a best man.

5. *Select your attendants.* The bride's sister is always her maid or matron of honor. If she has no sister of suitable age, she should choose her most intimate friend. Although it is not generally acceptable to have young married women as bridesmaids and an unmarried girl as maid of honor, this rule is broken in the case of a bride's unmarried sister.

The bridegroom usually asks his brother, brother-in-law, best friend, or father to serve as his best man. He then asks as many ushers as he will need to seat the guests in the church—usually one usher for every fifty guests. A married man may act as usher, or a married woman as matron of honor, but it is rare for a man and wife to serve at the same

wedding. The one not officiating is nevertheless invited to the wedding.

The bride and groom usually ask their attendants to serve in their wedding at the time the engagement is announced, or shortly thereafter. Bridesmaids pay for everything they wear except their floral bouquets which are presented to them by the bride. Ushers provide their own attire, too.

6. *Compile your wedding lists for the church, reception, and announcements.* Invitations to a large church wedding are never limited, and should be sent to all friends and relatives of both families, regardless of whether they can be present. Only a very small church or chapel would limit the number of guests invited to the ceremony. For a private ceremony, house wedding, or reception, where the guest list is limited, the bride's family may tell the groom's family how many guests they may invite. The number of each family is not always evenly divided. And it is traditional for the bride's family, who assume the expenses, to invite a higher proportion of the guests.

While drawing up your invitation lists for the ceremony and reception, you may compile a special list of people to receive announcements only. Remember, guests at house weddings are always invited to the reception as well as the ceremony, although for church weddings the number of guests may vary for the ceremony and reception. Announcements are sent only to friends who are *not invited* to the wedding.

7. *Order your wedding invitations and announcements,* as well as the personal stationery you will need for

wedding gift "thank you's." For pointers on wedding forms, see pages 19–25.

8. *Order your bridal gown, select gowns for the bridesmaids,* and urge the mothers to get together to choose their clothes. For details on wedding clothes, see pages 27–40.

9. *Arrange for floral decorations* for the church or ceremony, for the bride's and bridesmaids' bouquets, and for reception decorations after getting an estimate from your florist. For details on flowers for the wedding, see pages 57–64.

10. *Arrange for your wedding music* through your clergyman, sexton, or organist. For details on music for the ceremony and reception, see pages 65–66.

11. *Set a date with your photographer for your bridal portrait* and/or candid pictures of your wedding. See page 67 for details on photographs.

12. *Make transportation arrangements* for limousines or privately driven cars to take the wedding party and both sets of parents to the church. For a large church wedding, a policeman or parking attendant may be hired to help direct traffic and parking.

13. Begin to plan the décor of your new home or apartment, and to shop for your household trousseau as well as your personal trousseau.

Last Two Months Before the Wedding

Make your medical, dental and beauty shop appointments at appropriate times.

2. Select gifts for the groom and your bridesmaids.

3. Prepare for your bridesmaids' luncheon and set the date for your rehearsal dinner or party, if one is planned.

4. Register your silver, china, and crystal patterns with the Bridal Gift Registry in your favorite store.

5. Change your name on all important papers: driver's license, personal bank account, insurance policies.

6. Mail invitations so that they are received at least three weeks before the wedding.

7. Record all wedding gifts and mail your "thank you" notes as soon as each gift is received.

8. Make hotel or housing reservations for your attendants.

9. List what items you still need for your new household; make moving arrangements if necessary.

10. Prepare a list of things you will need for your honeymoon and begin to pack them in your luggage.

11. Set up your gift display shelves or table if you plan to display your wedding gifts.

12. Set aside everything you will use and wear on your wedding day and keep it together, in one place; check

bridesmaids' apparel and accessories to be sure costumes are complete.

13. Make final arrangements with your caterer, florist, photographer, church secretary or sexton on any last minute changes.

14. Send out wedding announcements

When the wedding is given by the bride's father, and her mother is still living, the second wife does not go to the church and the bride's mother does not attend the reception. The bride's mother sits in the front pew with members of her family (but not her second hus-

Emily Post's Pointers to the Bride

The loveliest rule in planning your wedding is still: "Whatever you do, do exquisitely!"

Expert advice from a professional caterer, florist, photographer, or bridal consultant is never an extravagance and can save you costly mistakes.

and glossies of your pictures to society editors.

15. Write out place cards for bride's table, if there is to be one.

16. Relax and get ready to enjoy the most glorious wedding day ever!

A Note About Divorced Parents of the Bride

When divorced parents are on friendly terms, both parents and step-parents come to the church and to the reception. The one unbreakable ban is the sending of a joint wedding invitation by the divorced parents. This is never acceptable.

When parents are not friendly, the wedding is given by the bride's mother. The bride's father may drive with her to the church and escort her down the aisle, but he does not attend the reception. He may, of course, have his own small reception for the bride and groom after the mother's reception.

band). After the bride's father gives his daughter away, he takes his place in one of the pews behind his ex-wife.

Duties of the Bride's Attendants

The maid or matron of honor holds the bride's bouquet during the ceremony and adjusts the bride's veil before the recessional. She also signs the marriage certificate and helps the bride change into her going-away ensemble after the reception. She may also help the bride address wedding invitations, inform members of the bridal party about rehearsal plans, and entertain for the bride at a pre-wedding party or shower. She pays for her own wedding costume, provides her own transportation to the bride's home or church, and sends a wedding gift to the bridal couple.

The other bridal attendants are expected only to be punctual at rehearsal, pretty at the wedding, and provide their own transportation to and from the church or bride's home. They, too, pay for their own ensembles and send a gift to the bride.

Duties of the Best Man

The best man—the groom's brother, father, or closest friend—plays an important role in the wedding, particularly the formal wedding. As secretary, valet, and general Man Friday to the groom, the best man is traditionally responsible for everything required by the groom. He sees to it that the groom's wedding clothes are ordered, as well as all boutonnières, and that the groomsmen appear at the rehearsal on schedule. He also carries the marriage license, the wedding ring, and clergyman's fee to the church, sees that the groom is in the vestry thirty minutes before the ceremony and that the ushers are at the church a full hour before the ceremony or forty-five minutes before the home wedding.

After the ceremony, the best man joins in the recessional, escorting a maid or matron of honor, and then takes up his duties concerning the couple's luggage. At the reception, he proposes the first toast to the bride and groom and reads the congratulatory telegrams. When the bride and groom are ready to leave, he collects both sets of parents and other close relatives for the final farewell and sees that the "get-away" car is brought around in time. With the maid of honor, he then clears a path through the guests for the bride and groom to depart amid the traditional shower of confetti and rice.

Duties of the Ushers

The ushers—still called "groomsmen" in many parts of the country—have a definite function at a church wedding.

Their role is often merely honorary at a home wedding where there is seldom any formal seating and where standards and ribbons mark the standing area. The head usher, however, takes the bride's mother up the aisle. After the ceremony the ushers remove the ribbons and standards.

At a church wedding, the ushers arrive one hour before the ceremony and receive the boutonnières, gloves, and ties provided by the groom. Each usher receives a guest list assigned to the reserved pews. As women guests arrive, ushers ask whether they are friends of the bride or friends of the groom, offering their right arm, and then escorting them to the left or the right. If several guests arrive at the same time, the ushers seat the eldest lady first. The others may either follow singly, or await the return of another usher.

After the head usher has escorted the bride's mother to the front left-hand pew, the ushers roll down the aisle canvas or carpet, if one is used, and draw the ribbons. The bride's mother is the last to be seated, and after her entry, other guests seat themselves quietly at the back. Ushers should always be dignified and poised. Their conversation with guests should be gracious but not too exuberant.

After the recessional, the ushers return to escort all the ladies in the reserved pews to the door. The bride's mother goes first, then the groom's mother, eldest ladies, and so forth until all of the members of the families have left the church. The ushers then remove the ribbons, see that the wedding party is driven to the reception, and arrange transportation for special guests, if necessary.

At the reception, ushers often assist elderly persons to the receiving line, introduce those who are alone, and dance with bridal attendants. As members of the wedding party, the "groomsmen" always give a gift to the bride, individually, or they contribute to a substantial, collective wedding gift.

A Note to the Parents of the Groom

The responsibilities and expenses of the parents of the groom are light and pleasant. They are required only to provide the bride's parents with a list of their wedding guests and to pay their own hotel bills if necessary. The groom's mother may get together with the mother of the bride to discuss wedding clothes. And she may also want to give a tea or "at home" to introduce the bride-to-be to her friends. Frequently the groom's parents offer to give the rehearsal dinner for the bridal party—a gay and intimate event in the repertoire of wedding festivities.

ding veil. For a bride's second marriage, however, simplicity is the rule.

The widow's wedding should be small and informal. She does not wear the bridal veil, orange blossoms, or myrtle (emblems of virginity), nor does she have more than one attendant, her maid or matron of honor. A wedding in best taste for a widow is held in a small church or chapel, or at home. Decorations are limited to a few flowers or some branched greens in the chancel. There are no ribboned-off seats, and no more than two ushers, if any, since only immediate families and very intimate friends are invited.

The bride wears an afternoon dress and hat of a color, or she may wear white. She usually wears a corsage, instead of carrying a bouquet. A family dinner, or the simplest of receptions, follows the ceremony.

The wedding of a widow is usually so small that invitations are extended by

A Note About the Second Marriage

The fact that the groom has been married previously has no effect on the wedding plans of his bride. Her status alone determines the formality of the wedding and whether or not she wears the wed-

personal notes from the bride or given verbally. However, if the bride is very young, and the wedding is of sufficient size, her parents may send out engraved forms. For details on the widow's invitation and announcement, see pages 6, 7, and 24.

3

Wedding Invitations and

Announcements

At the traditional wedding, friends are asked to the reception as well as to the ceremony and acquaintances are invited to the church ceremony only. If the wedding is small and private, guests are invited in person or by short notes. All friends and acquaintances not invited to the wedding usually receive announcements.

Once the wedding list is compiled, the date, time, and place of ceremony and reception set, the bride and her mother may order the invitations. Engraved invitations are ordered no later than two months in advance and sent out at least three weeks in advance to give guests sufficient notice. Handwritten invitations to a smaller wedding may be mailed as late as ten days before the wedding day.

Correct wedding invitations are always engraved in black on the first page of a double sheet of ivory or white note paper. The paper—either plain or with a raised margin called a platemark—should be of finest quality.

If the bride's family has a coat of arms, the insignia, or crest alone, may be embossed without color at top center of the sheet. Otherwise, the invitations bear no device of any kind.

The style of engraving may be chosen from many proper styles of lettering offered by a fine stationer. Graceful script is always in excellent taste.

Wedding Invitations and Types of Weddings

For the large, formal wedding, many engraved invitations are issued for both the church and the reception.

For the church wedding, followed by a small or private reception, many engraved invitations are issued to the ceremony, few to the reception.

For the private ceremony, followed by a large reception, there are no engraved invitations to the ceremony and many to the reception.

For the small, simple wedding—with or without reception—the bride and groom extend written or verbal invitations to the ceremony.

Mrs Frank Wilson Cross
requests the honour of your presence
at the marriage of her daughter
Marie Theresa
to
Mr Kenneth Chase Brooks
on Sunday, the tenth of July
at two o'clock
Saint Joseph's Church
New York

Mr. Pres
on Saturday, th
nineteen hund.
at hal

requ
at th

in

The favour
3708 Strath
Shaker Heig

Mr. and Mrs. William Howard
request the pleasure of your company
at the marriage of their daughter
Elizabeth
to
Mr. Gary Kenneth Butler
on Saturday, the twelfth o
at nine o'clock
The Waldorf-As
New Yor

Jack William James
honour of your presence
iage of her daughter
t Wynne
to
e Phelps, Jr.
-third of June
sixtu

Reception
ly following the ceremony
e church parlour
is requested
d

The Church Invitation

The proper invitation to the church ceremony reads:

> Mr. and Mrs. John Smith
> request the honor of your presence
> at the marriage of their daughter
> Mary Maude
> to
> Mr. Henry Blake Jones
> Tuesday, the fifth of June
> at four o'clock
> Trinity Church

The Invitation to the Reception

The invitation to the breakfast or reception following the church ceremony, engraved on a card to match the paper of the church invitation, reads:

> Mr. and Mrs. John Smith
> request the pleasure of
> (name written in)
> company at breakfast
> Tuesday, the fifth of June
> at half after twelve o'clock
> 43 Park Avenue

R.s.v.p.

Or, a small card is enclosed with the invitation to the church which reads:

> Reception
> immediately following the ceremony
> 43 Park Avenue

R.s.v.p.

The forms R.s.v.p. and R.S.V.P. are both correct. The former, however, is preferred by the conservative.

Wedding and Reception Invitation in One

For a country wedding, or parish reception, when everyone is invited to remain after the ceremony, the invitation to the reception or breakfast is added to the invitation to the ceremony. It reads:

and afterwards at breakfast
Bright Meadows
(or)
and afterwards at the reception
in the Parish House

Invitations to a Large Reception Following a Private Ceremony

When the ceremony is private and a large reception follows, the invitations to the ceremony are given in person or by phone, and invitations to the reception are sent out for a somewhat later hour. The wording for this invitation is:

Mr. and Mrs. John Smith
request the pleasure of
(name or names written in) *company*
at the wedding reception
of their daughter
Millicent Jane
and
Mr. Henry Strothers
Tuesday, the first of August
at half after twelve o'clock
555 Park Avenue
R.s.v.p.

Handwritten Invitations from the Bride

For a small wedding the bride writes her own invitations to her friends and family and those of the bridegroom. (Her mother writes to all other guests.) An informal invitation, written on plain white or off-white note paper marked with a home address, might read:

Dear Helen,
Dick and I are to be married at Christ Church Chantry at noon on Thursday, the tenth. We both want you and John to come to the church and afterward to breakfast at my aunt's, Mrs. Horace Jones, at 2 Park Avenue.
Hoping so much that you can be with us.
Affectionately,
Jane

Forms for Special Circumstances

When the bride is an orphan, three forms may be used. If the bride has no relatives and the wedding is given by friends, the wording is:

Mr. and Mrs. John Neighbor
request the honor of your presence
at the marriage of
Miss Elizabeth Orphan
to
Mr. John Henry Bridegroom
etc.

If she has brothers, the oldest one sends out her wedding invitations and announcements in his name. Or, if another relative has taken the place of a parent, his or her name is used. The bride may also send her invitations in her own name, using the following form:

The honor of your presence
is requested
at the marriage of
Miss Elizabeth Orphan
to
etc.

Or, she and the bridegroom may announce their own marriage this way:

Miss Elizabeth Orphan
and
Mr. John Henry Bridegroom
announce their marriage
etc.

Mr. and Mrs. John Weatherspoon
announce the marriage of their daughter
Barbara Betty
to
Mr. John Edgar Thomas
on Thursday, the twentieth of June
Nineteen hundred and fifty-nine
New York

Reception
ately following the ceremony
Essex House
160 Central Park South
New York

eply is requested
ery Street
ew York

When the bride's parents are divorced, and the bride does not live with her father, the invitations and announcements are sent out by the bride's mother and her present husband:

Mr. and Mrs. John Newhusband
request the honor of your presence
at the marriage of her daughter
Mary Brown
etc.

The double wedding invitation:

Mr. and Mrs. Henry Smartlington
request the honor of your presence
at the marriage of their daughters
Marian Helen
to
Mr. Judson Jones
and
Amy Caroline
to
Mr. Herbert Scott Adams
Saturday, the tenth of June
at four o'clock
Trinity Church

The elder sister's name is given first.

Mrs. Charles David Garrison
requests the honour of your presence
at the marriage of her daughter
Marjorie Theresa
to
Mr. Harold Jason Crawford
on Saturday, the twenty-second of June
at half after three o'clock
at the Church of the Good Shepherd
in the City of New York

The Widow's Invitation and Announcement

The young widow's invitation is sent in the name of her parents in the same style as the invitations for her first wedding. This time, however, her name instead of being written as Priscilla is written as Priscilla Banks Loring:

Mr. and Mrs. Maynard Banks
request the honor of your presence
at the marriage of their daughter
(or) *announce the marriage of their daughter*
Priscilla Banks Loring
etc.

Announcements

If no general invitations have been issued to the church, an announcement engraved on note paper like that of the invitation to the ceremony should be sent to friends of both the bride's and groom's families as soon after the wedding as possible.

If a marriage has been kept secret, announcements are sometimes sent out months later, but the actual marriage date should be included. The wording of the announcement is explicit:

Mr. and Mrs. John Smith
have the honor of announcing
(or) *the honor to announce*
the marriage of their daughter
Mary Maude
to
Mr. Henry Blake Jones
on Tuesday, the tenth of June
one thousand nine hundred and sixty-three
Cleveland, Ohio

The announcement of the marriage of a mature widow reads:

Mrs. Mary Hoyt
and
Mr. Worthington Adams
announce their marriage
on Monday, the second of November
one thousand nine hundred and fifty-five
at Saratoga Springs
New York

Emily Post's Points of Propriety

Announcements are never sent to those who have been invited to the wedding.

Invitations to a large wedding and reception are sent three to four weeks in advance.

Invitations should always be sent to the bridegroom's family (even when the families are intimate friends) and to members of the wedding party.

Engraved invitations and announcements are not in best taste for a divorcée.

Folding and Inserting

In preparing invitations for mailing, all of the envelopes are addressed first. *The tissue sheets which the engraver uses should be removed,* except where the ink is not thoroughly dry.

An envelope-size invitation is inserted in the inner envelope with the engraved side toward you. A larger invitation is folded in half with the engraving inside, and inserted—folded edge down—into the envelope. With the unsealed flap of this filled inner envelope in the palm of your hand, insert it in the mailing envelope.

To those who are only asked to the church, no house or reception invitation is enclosed.

Addressing

The mailing envelope is always addressed by hand to:

Mr. and Mrs. George W. Brown
26 Parkway
Home Town

In all formal correspondence, it is improper to abbreviate the state name, but it is correct to omit it when the invitations are posted for delivery in the same city, or when otherwise unnecessary. New York, for example, need never be written twice.

Envelopes should not be addressed:

Mr. and Mrs. James Greatlake and Family

The phrase "and Family" has never been considered in best taste. Miss Mary Greatlake or "The Misses Greatlake" may be written beneath the names of their parents on the mailing envelope, but a separate invitation should be sent to "The Messrs." All members of the family not living at the family's home address should receive separate invitations.

The names of children under twelve or thirteen are written on the inner envelope this way:

Priscilla, Penelope, Harold, and Jim

The inside envelope is addressed to Mr. and Mrs. Brown—*and nothing more* —unless the names of other members of the family are to be included.

Return addresses are not correct on invitations and announcements. However, when the address of a far-away friend is in doubt, it is permissible to put your address in the upper left corner of the envelope, so that it may be returned to you if the letter is not delivered.

Inviting the Clergyman

Unless the wedding is so small that there is no reception, the clergyman and his wife should always receive an invitation.

Recalling Wedding Invitations

When an engagement is broken off after the wedding invitations have been issued, the following form is correct:

Mr. and Mrs. Benjamin Nottingham
announce that the marriage of their daughter
Mary Katherine
to
Mr. Jerrold Atherton
will not take place

Cards are always printed instead of engraved for reasons of time.

4

Wedding Attire for the Bride and Members of the Wedding

Whether you have a large church wedding with ten bridesmaids, or a quiet home wedding with your sister at your side, you will look your loveliest on your wedding day. Your gown—as becoming as it can be—will set the note of formality for the wedding and the style of dress for the wedding party.

The Bridal Gown and Veil

At her first wedding, the bride wears a white gown and bridal veil whether she is sixteen or forty. The traditional bridal fabric is satin—heavier in winter, lighter in summer. Lace is also worn throughout the year. Fabrics for autumn and winter include faille, peau-de-soie, crêpe, velvet, silk alpaca, moire, taffeta, and opulent brocade. In midsummer,

chiffon, organdy, mousseline-de-soie, organza, dotted swiss, and the sheer cottons have their season, but only until mid-August when a silkier, swisher material is more suitable.

For a formal or semi-formal wedding, the gown is full length with a train, or floor length without a train. For informal weddings, gowns may be floor length or street length.

Many of today's bridal fashions follow the popular trend toward convertibility. Trains may be detached and jackets and bodices may be removed for "happily-ever-after" partying.

Virtually every detail—necklines, sleeves, or skirts—can be as individual as the bride, but the most elegant styles are simple and classic. Although white is traditional, the palest whispers of blue

or pink or ivory are often more flattering to the skin. And though a very young bride may look her loveliest in a cloud of white tulle, a mature bride in her thirties may choose the dignity of off-white satin or lace.

The Wedding Veil

Down through the ages, the wedding veil has been cherished as a unique symbol of bridal regalia. An emblem of virginity, the wedding veil is worn only at a first marriage.

Wedding veils of tulle or lace (or a fabric to match the gown) extend the full length of the train in a long, fluid sweep. Illusion face veils or fingertip veils also lend a lovely ethereal look. The face veil (worn with veils of varying length) is most appropriate for a very young bride. It may be mounted on a tiara, fastened to a cap or circlet of tiny flowers, or arranged on a headdress created by the bride herself.

The Bridal Train

The length of the train depends upon the size of the church, the height of the bride, and the style of the bridal gown. The very long train and veil are used only for large, formal weddings in a church or cathedral. Shorter chapel-length trains are more popular today for all types of weddings, including home and garden weddings. However, a bridal train is never used in a rectory wedding, regardless of the formality of the ceremony or the reception which follows.

Accessories and Make-up for the Bride

The bride's slippers are of white silk or satin. Stockings are pale and sheer, but never white. Gloves are not required for a small wedding, and are unnecessary if the bride's hands and forearms

are hidden by sleeves or by her bouquet. When elbow-length or long evening gloves are worn, two inches of the left glove's ring finger are ripped open for the ring ceremony. If short gloves are worn, the bride simply pulls off the glove at the altar.

Pale, colorless jewelry, such as a pearl necklace, gives the most elegant look to a wedding gown. Nonetheless, the bride always wears the jewel given to her by the bridegroom, regardless of color.

The bride's make-up should always be applied with a delicate touch. A painted, theatrical effect detracts from the bride's beauty and the dignity of the occasion. Suggestion and understatement are still the keys of beauty, particularly for a bride.

Bridal Attire for Informal Weddings

For an informal wedding, the bride may wear a face veil with a gown of ballerina length or of floor length. With a street dress or going-away suit, she usually wears a small hat or headdress. If a bride chooses to be married in a short costume, most appropriate for a mature bride or a second marriage, she may have only one attendant, her maid or matron of honor. The bride who has been married before does not wear white nor does she wear the wedding veil.

For a civil marriage in a judge's chambers or city hall, the bride wears a street-length dress or suit, a small hat, and a corsage.

Whatever costume the bride chooses, she may always wear "something old, something new, something borrowed, something blue," traditional amulets of bridal fortune.

Clothes for the Bridal Party

Bridesmaids' Costumes—gowns, slip-

pers, hose, bouquets, gloves, and head-dresses—are always selected by the bride and paid for by the bridesmaids. Taking their cue from the bridal gown, the ensembles of the bridal attendants are identical in style and fabric, although they may vary in color. A rainbow effect is lovely, with bridesmaids wearing graduated colors. The first two in American beauty, for example, the next two in a shade lighter, and so on down to the maid of honor in palest pink.

Other enchanting color schemes may be achieved with peach-color gowns and delphinium bouquets, chartreuse with wine yellow roses, or cool strawberry pinks with lilacs or purple tulips. Muted golds and burnt oranges are luscious for fall. And seasonal flowers and foliage may always be used for dramatic effects, particularly at holiday times.

The bridesmaids almost always carry flowers, bouquets, baskets, or sheaves which they hold on their outside arms. Those walking on the right side hold them on the right arm with the stems pointing downward to the left; those on the left hold their flowers on the left arm. Bouquets or baskets, however, are held in front.

Muffs in winter, summer fans or parasols, and flower-filled baskets all make charming accessories for the bridesmaid. Wreaths or garlands of flowers should match those in her basket or bouquet.

If gloves are worn, white kid is the loveliest in all lengths.

Slippers, in silk or satin, should be dyed in one lot to match the color of their gowns.

Emily Post's Points of Propriety

If the bride's gown is ballerina-length, the attendants' dresses must also be short. However, theirs may be short, even when the bride wears a long gown with a train.

Modern brides are usually mindful of their attendants' budgets and select a gown that lends itself to after-the-wedding use.

The dress of the maid or matron of honor is often similar but different in color and style from the bridesmaids' dresses. Her bouquet or basket may differ, too, but her ensemble should harmonize with both the bridal gown and the bridesmaids' costumes.

Junior Bridesmaids—young girl attendants between seven and fourteen years of age—wear modified copies of the bridesmaids' gowns.

Flower girls and pages—little girls and boys under seven—are dressed in quaint period costumes of white silk or satin. A page may also wear a dark Eton suit with a white boutonnière. The girl could also wear a pastel-colored party dress with a wreath and carry a bouquet.

The Ring Bearer—a small boy under seven—is always dressed in white. He carries the ring, deftly pinned or stitched on a small white cushion, and walks ahead of the bride.

For all informal weddings, bridal attendants wear clothes in keeping with the costume of the bride, the hour of the day, and the place of the wedding.

Emily Post's Point of Propriety

Nearest relatives of the bride and groom should not choose black unless they never wear another color. In this case, a touch of white or color should be added to the costume.

What the Best Man, Ushers, and Fathers Wear

It is correct for the best man and ushers to wear the same attire as the groom, with the exception of the boutonnières. Often the groom and best man wear ascots, and the ushers wear four-in-hands. Both fathers usually wear the same type of dress as the men in the wedding party.

The Pretty and Proper Look for the Mother-of-the-Bride

For a wedding between the hours of eight A.M. and six P.M., the mothers wear afternoon dresses in soft colors (never black) in an appropriate style and length. Simple, understated lines are most flattering. Hats and gloves are worn and usually flowers, although corsages are not a "must." In the receiving line, both mothers wear their hats and gloves.

For the evening wedding, full-length dinner dresses are in best taste. Heads and shoulders are always covered in church. Chiffon scarfs, veils, and flowers may be used as headdresses when evening hats are not in fashion. For a small wedding, when the bride wears a short dress or suit, the mothers wear the shorter length dress, as do the attendants. At a home wedding, hats are not necessary. Slippers are usually dyed to match the gowns.

Sisters, brothers, and grandparents of the bride and groom wear clothes similar to those worn by the parents. Children always wear their finest party clothes.

The Bridegroom's Wedding Apparel Chart

	DAYTIME	EVENING
Most formal:	Cutaway coat with waistcoat to match (or white) Striped trousers Stiff white shirt; wing collar Four-in-hand or bow tie (black and white, or gray) Black shoes and socks White boutonnière Black silk hat, gloves, and spats (optional)	Full dress (tail coat, stiff white shirt, wing collar, white lawn tie, white waistcoat) White evening gloves Black shoes and socks White boutonnière Black silk hat or opera hat
Less formal:	Black sack coat Gray or black Homburg hat with same accessories as those worn with cutaway coat	Tuxedo (White waistcoat optional) Black tie Patent leather oxford shoes White boutonnière Opera hat or black homburg; (panama or straw for summer)
Informal:	Dark blue suit White shirt with wing or stiff turn-down collar Blue and white tie, bow or four-in-hand White boutonnière Black shoes and socks	
Informal summer:	All white suit, or dark trousers and light jacket; or light trousers and dark jacket White boutonnière Black or navy blue tie	

5

The Bridal Shower and
Pre-Wedding Parties

Although their looks and manners tend to change with the years, the parties for the bride and her attendants are always sparkling, sentimental occasions. The bridal shower, so practical and popular in some communities, is needless for the bride with "the best of everything." But the charming custom lingers on, often in luncheons for the bride or joint showers for the bride and groom. The "bridesmaids' luncheon," "bachelor dinner," and "rehearsal party," once traditional preludes for the large, formal wedding, are frequently dispensed with today.

Indeed, the whole round of pre-wedding parties varies with the type of wedding, the custom of the community, and the tastes and circumstances of the bride and groom. These glorious events are nonetheless a joy to all, whatever their style, and *yours for the making!*

The Bridal Shower

The setting for a bridal shower is "as you like it"—a luncheon, dinner, afternoon tea, evening snack, or morning coffee; the time: about a month before the wedding. It is usually given by an intimate friend or member of the bridal party; *never by the immediate family of the bride.* Since everyone who attends must bring a gift, it is considerate for prospective shower-givers to get together and arrange a single shower when the same friends will be invited.

Shower gifts are usually small and inexpensive and of less importance than wedding gifts. Invitations are either telephoned or written by hand on "informals," but printed stationers' cards are equally proper.

Although wedding presents are sent from the shop where they are purchased, shower gifts are always brought by hand and presented personally upon arrival. Frequently, however, the packages are taken at the door by the hostess and placed with the others on the reception table in another room. Gift cards should be enclosed to avoid the self-conscious "That's from me" as each present is unwrapped. When everyone expected has arrived, the bride may then open her packages, one by one, and thank each friend individually.

Tempting Fare for a Shower

Showers are always gay and fanciful, and even more so when the refreshments are ample and attractively served. Coffee and cake, punch and sandwiches, cider and doughnuts are all-time favorites. For a few tantalizing party and punch ideas, look over the recipes on the pages that follow.

Chicken and Rice Salad in Tomatoes

¼ cup corn oil
¼ cup vinegar
¼ cup finely chopped onion
1 tablespoon salt
2 teaspoons curry powder (optional)
⅛ teaspoon pepper
3 cups cooked rice
3 cups cubed, cooked chicken
2 cups chopped celery
¼ cup chopped green pepper
1½ cups mayonnaise
10 to 12 fresh, ripe tomatoes
Salad greens

Combine corn oil, vinegar, onion, salt, curry powder, and pepper. Add to rice. Toss lightly until seasonings are well mixed with rice. Place in refrigerator for about 1 hour.

Meanwhile peel tomatoes by first dipping them in boiling water. Skins will slip off easily. Remove stem ends and starting at the top, cut into fourths, cutting about ⅔ of the way down. Chill tomatoes.

After rice has marinated about 1 hour, add chicken, celery, green pepper, and mayonnaise; mix thoroughly. Fill tomatoes with chicken salad. Chill. Serve on salad greens. Makes 10 to 12 servings.

Ruby Red Punch

- 1 cup water
- ¾ cup sugar
- 3 quarts cranberry juice cocktail
- 1 (1 quart 14-ounce) can unsweet-
  ened pineapple juice
- 1 (12-ounce) can frozen lemonade
- ½ cup lime juice

Boil sugar and water together for 5 minutes. Cool. In punch bowl stir sugar syrup
with cranberry and pineapple juice. Add
thawed lemonade and number of cans of
water as stated on can. Stir in lime juice.
Add ice or ice mold. Makes 6½ quarts or
50 4-oz. cup servings.

Variation: Just before serving, add 2 quart
  bottles pale dry ginger ale. Makes 8½
  quarts or 60 4-oz. cup servings.

Cranberry Punch (for 50)

- 4 quarts cranberry juice cocktail
- 1 (46-ounce) can pineapple grapefruit
  drink
- 1 quart ginger ale

Combine ingredients just before serving
over ice.

Wedding Cake Potato Salad

10 pounds potatoes

1 cup (8-ounce bottle) Italian corn oil dressing

2 quarts chopped celery

2 cups chopped onion

2 tablespoons salt

1 teaspoon white pepper

1 quart real mayonnaise

Tomatoes

Celery leaves

Cucumber slices

Real mayonnaise (for garnish)

Cook potatoes just until tender. Peel, dice, and toss with Italian corn oil dressing while still warm. Let marinate in refrigerator about 2 hours. Combine potatoes, celery, onion, salt and pepper. Add real mayonnaise and toss until well mixed. Line bottom and sides of 3 tier pans (10 x 2 inches, 8 x 2 inches, and 6 x 2 inches) with waxed paper. Firmly pack with potato salad. Cover. Chill several hours.

Uncover 10-inch layer. Invert serving plate over pan and turn upright, holding pan firmly against center of plate. Place on flat surface. Remove pan and waxed paper. Turn out 8-inch layer on center of large layer and 6-inch layer on top of all without lifting serving plate. (Remove waxed paper as each layer is unmolded.)

Garnish base of salad with tomato roses (directions below) and celery leaves. Circle base of middle layer with cucumber cups filled with real mayonnaise (directions below). Stand cucumber half slices and tomato points around base of top layer. Decorate top with a tomato rose and celery leaves. Makes about 8 quarts salad, 42 (¾ cups) servings.

To Make Each Tomato Rose: Peel tomato with vegetable peeler, starting at top and peeling around and around to bottom of to-

mato. Roll peeling around itself into rose shape.

To Make Each Filled Cucumber Cup: Make a cut from center through outer edge

2 bottles Champagne, chilled
1 to 2 quarts orange sherbet
Garnish: Fresh mint sprigs

of thin cucumber slices. Overlap edges, forming cup. Place on salad, overlapped edges down. Force real mayonnaise through pastry tube into cucumber cup.

Champagne Sherbet Punch

1 (6-ounce) can frozen orange concentrate
2 bottles Sauterne, chilled

Place frozen orange juice in punch bowl. Pour in chilled wine. Stir well to blend. At serving time, pour in champagne, then add sherbet by spoonfuls. Serve in small punch glasses, topped with mint or thin slices of lime. Makes about 40 punch cup servings.
Notes: Block of ice in punch bowl may be omitted because of using frozen juice and sherbet. Shortcut: To save last-minute flurry, freeze scoops of sherbet in advance of party. Merely spoon sherbet on flat dish or baking sheet, store in freezer until needed.

SUMMER SHOWER
FOR BRIDE-TO-BE
Pineapple-Lemon Party Punch
Raspberry Ripple Ice Cream Pie
Creamy Mints
Party Nut Cups

Minted Strawberry-Lemon Tea Punch
(MAKES 3½ QUARTS)

1 cup water

2 tablespoons loose green tea or 6 tea bags

2 large sprigs fresh mint

2 cups water

2 cups sugar

1½ cups fresh lemon juice

1 pint fresh, frozen, or canned strawberry or cranberry juice

2 quarts ice water or carbonated water

Few drops red food coloring

Bring water to vigorous boil; add tea and crushed mint leaves. Remove from heat; cover and steep 5 minutes. Stir, then strain into large punch bowl or container. Make a syrup by boiling 2 cups water and sugar for 10 minutes. Cool. Blend all ingredients together.

Emily Post's Points of Propriety

The bridal shower is never given by the bride's mother, sister, or any member of her immediate family.

Whether or not a wedding present is sent in addition to a shower gift depends upon the custom of the community. It also depends upon how well one knows the bride and how much one can afford to spend.

Ideas for Bridal Showers
Kitchen gadgets   Notions
Gourmet items and cookbooks
Soaps and cosmetics
Linens and lingerie

Ideas for Joint Showers
Individual small items for "him" and for "her"
Pairs of items—monogrammed "His" and "Hers"
Books and stationery
Garden supplies
Hobby and game equipment

The Bachelor Dinner

This festive dinner is usually held two or three nights before the wedding at the home of the groom's parents, or at a club or hotel. Traditionally, it is the occasion when the groom bids farewell to his bachelorhood with those who have been his close companions. It is a gay and happy farewell—but not the wild, ribald affair often reported.

In the time-honored custom, the groom rises, lifting a champagne-filled glass "To the Bride." His guests respond with rising toasts, as the groom smashes his glass in the fireplace or breaks the delicate stem of the goblet.

All guests follow suit, symbolizing the final toast from those goblets.

Boutonnières are sometimes put at each place, as well as the groom's gifts to his groomsmen, unless it is more convenient to present them later.

The Bridesmaids' Luncheon

Among the warmest and most intimate of pre-wedding parties is the occasion when the bride entertains her bridesmaids and presents them with their gifts. A tea, dinner, or buffet supper are all charming alternates for the traditional bridesmaids' luncheon. The table is often decorated with bridesmaids' roses or flowers that echo the color scheme of the wedding. A fine lace, linen, or organdy luncheon cloth, fine china and crystal add to the grace of the table. The gifts—attractively wrapped and tagged—also add a festive touch to each place setting.

Before the wedding, it is customary for the maid-of-honor, the bridal attendants, and other intimate friends to entertain the bride. A small luncheon or buffet, similar in style to the bridesmaids' luncheon, is most popular. A few suggested menus follow.

SIMPLE LUNCHEON
Turkey Jelly Ring
Grapes
Hot Potato Salad
Fruit-Nut Cream
Coffee

Turkey Ring

   2 envelopes unflavored gelatin
   ¼ cup cold water
   3 bouillon cubes
  3¼ cups boiling water
   2 tablespoons lemon juice
   1 tablespoon grated onion
   3 cups cooked turkey pieces
  1⅓ cups finely diced celery
   3 tablespoons finely chopped parsley
   1 cup real mayonnaise
   ½ pound seedless grapes
   ½ pound tokay grapes
    Chicory

Sprinkle gelatin on cold water; let soften five minutes. Add softened gelatin and bouillon cubes to boiling water in bowl; stir until completely dissolved. Mix in lemon juice and onion. Overlap larger pieces of turkey in bottom of 2-quart ring mold. Pour in enough gelatin mixture to cover slices; chill until firm. Chill remaining gelatin until mixture reaches consistency of unbeaten egg white. Fold remaining turkey, celery, parsley, and mayonnaise into thickened gelatin. Spoon on top of turkey layer in mold. Chill until firm. Unmold onto serving plate. Garnish with grapes and chicory. Serve with additional mayonnaise, if desired. Makes 12 servings.

Note: 2 (12-ounce) cans turkey may be used instead of fresh cooked turkey.

Fruit-Nut Cream

   2 envelopes unflavored gelatin
   ¼ cup cold water
   1 (1 pound 13-ounce) can fruit cock-
     tail
   1 pint heavy cream
  24 regular size marshmallows, cut in
     eighths
   1 cup broken pecans

Sprinkle gelatin on cold water to soften. Drain fruit; bring juice to boil, then remove from heat. Add softened gelatin and stir until completely dissolved. Chill until mixture reaches the consistency of unbeaten egg white. Whip cream; fold in drained fruit, marshmallows, pecans, and chilled gelatin. Chill 6 to 8 hours. Makes 10 to 12 servings.

LUNCHEON FOR THE BRIDE-TO-BE
Molded Chicken Salad
Heart-shaped Sandwiches
Apricot Soufflé
Coffee

Wedding Bell Salad

    1 package lime flavored gelatin
    1 envelope unflavored gelatin
    ¼ cup cold water
    1 cup boiling water
    2 tablespoons lemon juice
    2 teaspoons grated onion
    ¾ teaspoon salt
    1½ cups diced cooked chicken
    1¼ cups canned crushed pineapple,
        well drained
    ¾ cup finely diced celery
    ⅓ cup finely diced pimiento
    1 cup real mayonnaise
    ½ cup heavy cream, whipped
    1 head chicory or lettuce
    Real mayonnaise

Prepare lime-flavored gelatin according to directions on package. Pour into 9-inch square pan. Chill until firm. Meanwhile, sprinkle unflavored gelatin on cold water. Let soften about 5 minutes, then add to boiling water in bowl and stir until completely dissolved. Mix in lemon juice, grated onion, and salt. Chill until mixture reaches the consistency of unbeaten egg white. Combine chicken, pineapple, celery, and pimiento and add to thickened gelatin; then fold in mayonnaise and whipped cream. Turn into 9-inch square pan. Chill until firm.

Cut molded chicken salad into 3-inch squares and cut lime-flavored gelatin with bell-shaped cutter. Arrange chicken squares and chicory on individual plates. Top each square with gelatin bell and pipe mayonnaise around edge of bell. Makes 9 servings. *Note:* 1 (12-ounce) can chicken may be used instead of fresh cooked chicken.

Cranberry Sparkler

    1 quart (4 cups) cranberry juice cock-
        tail
    2 cups orange juice
    4 (7-ounce each) bottles lemon-lime
        carbonated beverage

Pour ingredients over ice in punch bowl. Serve immediately. Garnish with scalloped orange slices. Makes 2½ quarts.

Sparkling Cranberry Punch

1 quart cranberry juice cocktail
1 quart champagne
1 pint pineapple or lemon sherbet

Just before serving, combine cranberry juice and champagne. Mix thoroughly. Pour over ice cubes in punch bowl and spoon sherbet on punch. Serves 16.

Pink Cooler

Pour equal parts of white muscatel and cranberry juice cocktail over ice cubes in punch bowl.

BRIDESMAIDS' LUNCHEON MENU

Fruit Sherbet Cocktail
Fish à la Newburg   Toast Cups
Molded Tomato Salad
French Dressing
Assorted Relishes
Bridesmaids' Cake
Beverage

Bridesmaids' Cake

2⅔ cups sifted flour
4 teaspoons baking powder
½ teaspoon salt
¾ cup corn oil or balanced oil margarine
¾ cup sugar
¾ cup light corn syrup
3 eggs
1 cup milk
1½ teaspoons vanilla

Sift flour, baking powder, and salt together three times. Cream margarine with sugar. Gradually beat in corn syrup, mixing until very light. Add eggs, one at a time, beating well after each addition. Combine milk and vanilla. Add dry ingredients alternately with milk mixture, beating just until mixed. Pour into greased, waxed paper lined, 13 x 9½ x 2-inch baking pan. Bake in 350°F. (moderate) oven until cake tests done, 40 to 45 minutes. Cool. Frost with Pink Satin Frosting.

Pink Satin Frosting

- 2 egg whites
- 1 cup red currant jelly
  - Dash salt
  - Red food coloring

Combine egg whites, jelly, and salt in double boiler top. Place over boiling water and beat mixture until jelly has melted. Remove from boiling water and continue beating until mixture is cool and fluffy. Tint desired shade with food coloring.

The Rehearsal or Bridesmaids' and Ushers' Dinner

This dinner, traditionally given to entertain the out-of-town members of the wedding party, is no longer fashionable today when the attendants often live in the same city where the wedding is to take place.

Actually, a tea, dinner, or buffet supper may be given before or after the wedding rehearsal by the bride's parents, the groom's parents, or any close relative who wishes to entertain for the couple. The affair is always an exciting one, but it is best not to make it a late party, if it is held on the eve of the wedding.

6

Flowers, Music, and Photographs for the Wedding

Hⁿow elegantly and exuberantly flowers echo the joy of a wedding—in the bride's bouquet or in a simple arrangement of branches at the altar. Floral decorations, although not essential to a ceremony or reception, create striking effects. Since ancient times, brides have carried flowers or worn garlands to symbolize the sacred ritual of marriage. Throughout the centuries this lovely tradition has endured.

A Word About Bouquets and Boutonnières

Today, the use of flowers in a wedding varies with the setting, religious faith, and taste of the bride. In cities where the bridegroom orders the bride's bouquet, a white orchid is often inserted at the center to be removed after the ceremony and used as the bride's going-away corsage.

Over the greater part of the country, however, the bride's parents order the bouquets for the bride and bridesmaids, as well as the floral decorations for the church. The bride's corsage bouquet, however, remains the responsibility of the groom. And in some communities, it is still customary for him to send corsages to the mothers and grandmothers.

The bridegroom always furnishes the boutonnières for the best man, his ushers, and himself. The bride's father, unless he is a widower, receives his boutonnière from his own "bride," the bride's mother.

Apart from the bouquets and boutonnières for the bridal party, no other flowers are necessary. A profusion of flowers takes away from the gowns and the bouquets of the wedding party. But a few subtle touches of smilax, greenery, or flowers are significant, and therefore beautiful.

The Bridal Bouquet

For a formal wedding, the bride carries either a bouquet of white flowers or a small prayerbook. The prayerbook is often adorned with white streamers and tiny white flowers, or a single white orchid which doubles as the bride's going-away corsage.

For a very informal wedding where the bride is married in an afternoon dress or suit, a corsage is usually worn, although a small bouquet is equally proper.

A wide variety of flowers are suitable for the bride's bouquet. Beautiful designs—to suit the style and formality of the bridal gown—may be created from: *orchids, stephanotis, lilies of the valley, roses, gardenias, calla lillies, violets, lilacs, large white pansies, snapdragons, gladioli, sweet peas, daisies,* and other flowers.

To be sure of a pretty bouquet, choose a florist whom you can rely on, show him the style and material of your gown, and then give his artistry free rein.

Bouquets for the Bridesmaids

Bouquets of the bridal attendants are usually identical and fashioned to carry out the effect of their gowns. Old-fashioned arm-bouquets (carried in both arms, and all pointed in the same direction) are most suitable with long gowns. Decorated muffs, fans, and parasols with ribbons are also charming accessories. For spring and summer weddings, bridesmaids often wear floral wreaths or headdresses to match their bouquets.

As a rule, the bouquets complement the costumes in style and color. Smaller bouquets are used with shorter gowns; corsages with street clothes. The flower girl carries a basket of rose petals or a small nosegay.

The Boutonnières

Traditionally, the groom uses a spray from the bride's bouquet, lily-of-the-valley, or any tiny flower that is in season. Stephanotis is also appropriate for the groom's boutonnière which differs from the others. The best man and both fathers wear gardenias; the ushers carnations.

Floral Decorations for the Church

Flowers and greens of all varieties may be used to decorate the church when permitted by the clergyman. White and green is the traditional color scheme, although a garden of seasonal flowers, shrubs, and flowering branches may be selected for color and fragrance.

For a large church wedding, the altar, choir stalls, pew ends, aisle posts, and window recesses may all be exquisitely decorated. For a small, informal wedding, floral arrangements or vases and candelabra are placed in the chancel. Except at the altar, candles are used only after sundown.

A fine, reputable florist will probably know the setting's requirements and suggest the most effective decoration for the amount you wish to spend. He will also provide pew ribbons for the reserved section and the aisle carpet, if you want them. The pulling of the white ribbons and laying of the white carpet heighten the drama of the processional, and for large weddings prove to be practical as well as elegant appointments.

Flowers for the Home Wedding

A fireplace banked with greens or flowering shrubs makes a lovely background for both the ceremony and receiving line. Added touches of color may be created with a few well-placed floral arrangements. Introduce a breathtaking bouquet of American Beauty roses with bunches of grapes, or a single flowering branch with a few choice peonies. Even a simple staircase takes on elegant airs when bedecked with a row of potted "mums" and ivy sprays.

A kneeling bench or *prie dieu*—cushioned in white and trimmed with flowers—is often used without any suggestion of an altar. When an altar is desired, however, one may be adapted from a console table covered with a white cloth and decorated with flowers and candelabra.

For a Rectory Wedding or Civil Ceremony

Floral decorations are never furnished by the bride for a wedding in a parish house, judge's chambers, or municipal building. At a chapel ceremony, however, a few flowers may be used at the altar.

For the Reception

The backdrop of the receiving line is usually decorated with urns or baskets of flowers, dwarf trees, greens, or cande- labra. Floral centerpieces, candelabra, and lighted candles are used on small tables and on the large bride's table or buffet table.

The silver cake knife—used to cut the wedding cake—is gaily tied with tiny white flowers and streamers.

For Outdoor Weddings

A garden wedding may be simple or elaborate in decoration and appointments. Porch enclosures, canvas tents, or terrace awnings are frequently used to provide additional space for guests in an artistic setting. Smilax or greens make decorative covers for the central pole of a marquee, and stunning effects can be created with dogwood or wistaria. It is even possible to put an entire floor board under a marquee, but this is expensive and unnecessary. Canvas or carpet or even green grass are all excellent ground covers. If a wedding breakfast or "tea" is served in the tent, tables are decorated with small vases of flowers and candles.

Emily Post's Point of Propriety

Paper flowers or plastic flowers are never considered in fine taste for weddings.

Music for the Wedding Ceremony

Most symbolic, perhaps, of all the emotion and sentiment, solemnity and gaiety entwined in the marriage ceremony, is Wagner's stirring "Wedding March" from *Lohengrin*. Familiarly known as "Here Comes the Bride," its strains have become part of the beauty of the procession. Equally impressive and customary for the recessional is the "Wedding March" from Mendelssohn's *Midsummer Night's Dream*.

Both of these beloved classics may be played on the church organ, or by an orchestra, string ensemble, or record player for a home or garden wedding. Since many churches have restrictions,

all selections should be cleared with the clergyman or church musical director before plans are completed. Where these wedding marches are unacceptable, a hymn or non-secular triumphal march may be played on the organ or sung by the choir.

Choice religious works include:

"Praise, My Soul, the King of Heaven"
by Lyte
"Jesu, Joy of Man's Desiring" by Bach
"The Voice That Breathed O'er Eden"
by Hayden
Chorale Prelude: "In Thee Is Joy"
by Caravaggio
"The King of Love My Shepherd Is"
by Hinsworth
"Ave Maria" by Schubert
"Dreams" by Wagner
"Serenade" by Schubert
"Evening Star" by Wagner
"Songs" by Brahms
"Liebestraum" by Liszt
"The Swan" by Saint-Saëns
"Romance" by Debussy
"Salut d'Amour" by Elgar

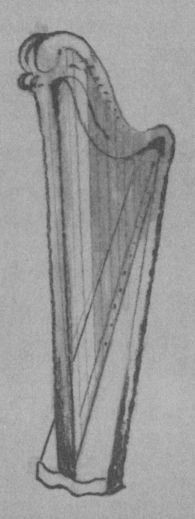

Solo selections for the ceremony:

"At Dawning" by Cadman
"O Perfect Love" by Barnby
"The Lord's Prayer" by Malotte
"The Voice That Breathed O'er Eden"
"I Love You Truly" by Carrie Jacobs
 Bond

Most churches permit a wide range of music, but it is tasteful to choose accepted classics.

Although music is not essential for a reception, it adds a contagious note of gaiety to the celebration. A guitarist, accordionist, or pianist is popular as soloist, and a trio, string ensemble, or full orchestra are best for dance music. While the guests are on the receiving line, the music is limited to semi-classical or light operatic selections; afterwards, favorite show tunes and popular music are played and sung by the musicians. For special request numbers, consult your soloist or orchestra leader.

Wedding Photographs

Among the bride's most treasured mementoes are her wedding photographs. And memory-making photographs require a *professional photographer* who should be engaged as far ahead of time as possible.

Formal photographs of the bride, sometimes called "bridal portraits," are usually taken well in advance of the wedding day at a photographic studio, or at a bridal salon with lighting facilities. An artificial replica of the bride's bouquet, or an actual duplicate, may be ordered from the florist for the photograph. During the photographic session, the bride's make-up should be soft and light to produce the loveliest effect.

If a bridal photograph is to accompany the wedding announcement, the photographer should be instructed to make an 8" x 10" glossy print for each society editor.

Pictures of the church, house, or table decorations are always taken before the ceremony, together with a few "portraits" of the bride, alone or with her bridesmaids. If you wish to be photographed in the church, or at the altar during the ceremony, permission should be obtained from your clergyman.

Today, the wedding album of candid photos has reached a new peak of popularity. Unreeling the complete story of the wedding day, these candid pictures capture such sentimental highlights as the cutting of the cake, the throwing of the bouquet, and the farewell shower of confetti and rice. The candid photographer can also pose the bride and groom formally and get pictures of them alone. After the proofs are submitted, they can then select those they want for their album, and those they may wish to have enlarged.

Formal or candid photographs of the bridal party are not generally presented as gifts to attendants. If the bridesmaids or ushers wish to have a wedding photograph, it is proper for them to order their own prints from the photographer.

Emily Post's Pointers to the Bride

It is safer and wiser to engage a professional photographer than to rely on a dearly beloved "amateur" to take your once-in-a-lifetime wedding pictures.

Warn your photographer not to delay the receiving line by taking too many pictures at this time.

7

The Word on Wedding Gifts

The gay, happy world of the engaged couple seems to spin and swirl in a galaxy of gifts. There are the wedding gifts to the bridal couple, their gifts to the attendants, and most important of all, the sentimental wedding gifts, exchanged between them.

The Wedding Rings

The bride's wedding ring, engraved with her initials and those of her groom (his first), and the momentous date, is her most cherished gift. She may also choose to give him a ring, marked in similar style, but with her initials preceding.

Gifts to the Groom

If the bride wishes to give the groom a gift other than a wedding band, or in addition to it, she chooses something permanent and handsome for his personal use. A watch, cuff links, or a smartly fitted traveling case are all useful and important gifts.

The Groom's Present to the Bride

According to tradition, the groom buys the finest gift he can afford as a lifetime treasure for his bride. Whether it is the simplest bangle or charm, an exquisite string of pearls, or a diamond pendant, it is always something for her personal adornment.

Gifts for the Bridesmaids

To show her appreciation of their services and to commemorate the occasion, the bride traditionally presents each of her attendants with a gift. The most popular bridesmaids' present is jewelry. The bride might also choose a silver tray or picture frame, engraved with the initials of the bride and groom and date of the wedding.

The gift to the maid or matron of honor need not be identical to the bridesmaids' gifts. Clocks and compacts, perfume bottles and picture frames, luggage and leather goods are all lovely choices

for attendants.

Gifts should be gaily wrapped and tagged with the name of each bridesmaid, and presented at the bridesmaids' luncheon, rehearsal dinner, or at any other appropriate time before the wedding.

Ushers' Gifts

The bridegroom's gifts to his ushers are presented at the bachelor dinner, wedding rehearsal, or immediately preceding the wedding. Cuff links are the most popular gifts. Silver or gold pencils, belt buckles, key rings, cigarette cases, billfolds, or other small, personal articles are also suitable.

The present to the best man may be the same as the ushers' gifts or even more handsome. Ushers are often presented with the gloves and neckties which they will wear at the wedding, or with articles engraved with their initials, the initials of the groom, and the date of the wedding.

Presents for Flower Girls and Ring Bearers

All the members of the bridal party are remembered with gifts, including the children. An appealing gift for a little girl might be a tiny charm, locket, or pendant; for a little boy, a manly coin case or key ring, books or sporting goods.

The Gifts to the Bride and Groom

Soon after the wedding invitations are mailed, the hectic household of the bride is deluged with gifts. The simplest way to keep track of "who sent what" is to keep a written record. Many brides have adopted the easy and effective system of numbering each gift (with a paste-on sticker) and then recording that number in their gift book, together with the name of the sender and date. (If you don't already have a bride's gift book, you may wish to use the Bride's Gift List at the back of this book on page 107.)

The rule on returning gifts is this: Gifts are never returned when a wedding is postponed, but if the wedding is called off, all are returned.

Exchanging Wedding Presents

A time-honored custom permits the bride to exchange all duplicate presents.

However, she never exchanges the presents chosen for her by her own family or by the bridegroom's family, unless expressly told she may do so.

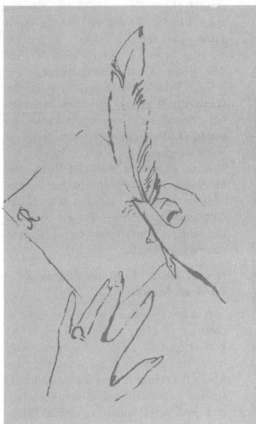

The Bride's Thanks

In return for the many presents showered upon the bride, there is a corresponding task which must not be evaded. The bride sends each gift-sender a short, handwritten note of thanks on the day each present arrives, if at all possible.

The note should always mention the specific gift that was sent. If for some reason, you don't know what the article is, or what function it serves, you may refer to it as "the lovely piece of china, silver, or crystal." In your thank-you note for a check, it is gracious to mention some item of permanent value that you and your groom plan to buy with the money.

When a present is sent by a married couple, the bride writes to the wife and thanks both. "Thank you for the lovely (item) you and Mr. Jones sent me." Or, she may begin her letter, "Dear Mr. and Mrs. Jones, Thank you both, etc. . . ."

The bride's thank you for an exchanged gift always mentions the original present sent, unless she knows the sender well enough to let him know she is exchanging it.

Most important, notes of thanks can be short, but they should be prompt. Many a bride who does not respond immediately often finds herself spending her entire honeymoon on this time-consuming detail.

Never, Never Send an Engraved Card of Thanks!

A flagrant affront to the tradition of common courtesy is the printed or engraved card of thanks. It is inexcusably rude! In the event of a hurried marriage where the couple must leave immediately for any reason, the bride's mother or sisters send brief notes explaining "Mary had gone when your lovely present arrived. She will, of course, write you as soon as she receives it." If it is not practical to forward the gift, her mother should write a description from which the bride may write her personal thank-you, mentioning the specific article.

Displaying the Wedding Gifts

While many of today's brides omit the wedding gift display, it is still customary and proper. However, the bridal gift display must always be at the bride's home and must always include *all of the gifts* she has received.

Gifts should be attractively arranged according to color, style, and value, so that each is shown to best advantage. The entire display may be set up on one large table or on card tables, elegantly covered with cloths of lace, damask, or organdy.

China is usually arranged in one grouping, silver in another, crystal in another, linens in another. Duplicates should never be shown together, and an inexpensive gift should not be placed next to an elaborate one. Regardless of where the gifts are displayed (any room from finished basement to bedroom is suitable), the effect should be artistic.

Displaying Checks

Gifts of money are not usually displayed. However, in fairness to the relatives or friends who sent checks instead of gifts, it is quite proper to display checks in overlapping fashion so that the amounts are concealed and the signatures alone disclosed. A square of glass is placed over the arrangement to keep the curious from handling.

A Note About Gift Cards

There is no definite rule on gift cards for the display. Many prefer to remove them, but there is no impropriety in leaving them on the gifts. The signed cards often save the family from answering countless questions about "who sent what."

8

The Wedding Ceremony

Marriage, the oldest tradition of all, has always been marked by impressive ceremony. The vows are exchanged in a service of deep spiritual significance. And it is important that your wedding echo the dignity and beauty of this hallowed ritual.

Formal Wedding Procedure

A formal wedding must proceed smoothly to achieve a perfect performance. A rehearsal, directed by the clergyman, sexton, or organist with all participants present, is therefore essential.

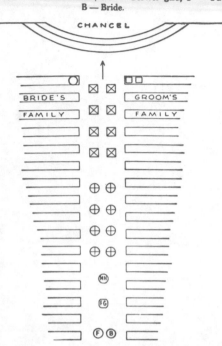

Formation of the wedding procession. Key: ⊠ — Ushers; ⊕ — Bridesmaids; MH — Maid of honor; FG — Flower girl; F — Father; B — Bride.

At a perfectly managed wedding, the bride arrives exactly one minute after the hour in order to give the last guest time to find a seat. No one should be seated after the entrance of the bride's mother. At this point the aisle canvas is put down, if one is used, and the ribbons hung. Guests who arrive late must stand in the vestibule or go into the gallery.

At the sound of the wedding march, the clergyman enters the chancel, followed by the groom and the best man. The groom stands on the right-hand side at the head of the aisle. The best man remains directly behind and to the right of the groom.

From the vestibule of the church the bridal procession moves down the aisle, headed by the ushers in pairs. Next come the bridesmaids, also two by two, in order of height. Then comes the maid (or matron) of honor, alone. The flower girls,

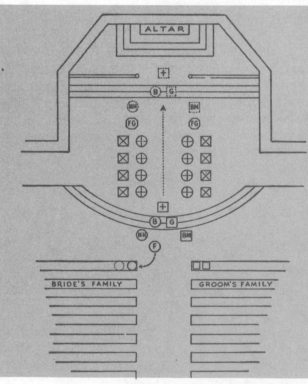

Group at the altar. Key: + — Minister; B — Bride; G — Groom; MH — Maid of honor; BM — Best man; FG — Flower girl; ⊠ — Ushers; ⊕ — Bridesmaids; F — Father of the bride.

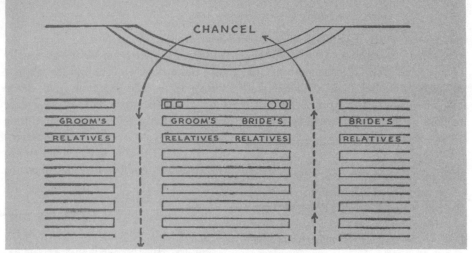

followed by the ring bearer come next, if they are included. Last of all comes the bride on the right arm of her father.

During the ceremony, the maid of honor stands at the left and slightly back of the bride and holds the bride's bouquet, as well as her own. At the conclusion of the ceremony, she hands back

groom, ring bearer, flower girl, maid of honor, bridesmaids, and ushers. At an ultra-formal wedding, the best man does not walk down the aisle with the maid of honor. He goes back into the vestry with the clergyman and gives him his fee, entrusted to him beforehand by the groom.

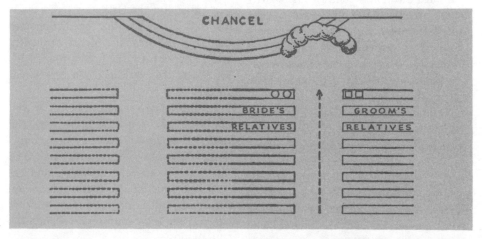

the bridal bouquet. Then as the bride turns to leave the chancel, she stoops and straightens out the bride's train, handing her own bouquet to a bridesmaid or laying it for a moment on the floor. Recovering her own bouquet, she follows the bride in the recessional.

The order of recessional is exactly the reverse of the processional: Bride and

The Double Wedding

At a double wedding the two bridegrooms follow the clergyman and stand side by side, each with his best man behind him, the groom of the older sister near the aisle. The ushers—friends of both bridegrooms—go up the aisle together. Then come the bridesmaids of the older sister followed by her maid of honor, who walks alone. The older sister follows on the right arm of her father. Then come the bridesmaids of the younger sister, her maid of honor, and last, the younger sister on the arm of a brother, uncle, or nearest male relative.

Immediately after the ceremony the bride and groom proceed to the reception. If the wedding breakfast or dinner is private, and many friends and neighbors are invited to the church only, it is gracious and proper for the bride and groom to wait at the back of the church and receive the good wishes of these guests as they file out.

The Roman Catholic Wedding

Roman Catholic weddings customarily center around the Nuptial Mass, celebrated between eight A.M. and noon. Hence, arrangements must be made at the rectory several months in advance. The banns are usually proclaimed from the pulpit and posted on the church calendar p.ior to the wedding. The couple should therefore complete their church arrangements before making any reception plans. It is also recommended, though not obligatory, that the Catholic members of the bridal party receive Holy Communion at the Nuptial Mass, at which guests receiving the invitation to do so may also participate.

Whether the bride and groom and best man and maid of honor, or the entire bridal party are permitted within the altar rail is determined by individual church practice. Since some churches have strict rules about the social accompaniments of the wedding, it is essential that the couple check these restrictions in advance.

Although afternoon weddings usually take place between four and five o'clock, they may be held any time from one to six. A Catholic wedding may take place any time during the year; but during the closed seasons of Lent and Advent the Nuptial Blessing is not given, unless permission is granted by the bishop.

The Jewish Ceremony

Orthodox and Reform Jewish weddings differ from one another only in the ceremony. In the Orthodox ceremony, the bride is veiled and escorted under a canopy (*chupah*) by her father and mother. The groom is also escorted by his parents. Hats are worn by all men attending the ceremony. Within recent years, the *chupah* has been made stationary behind the altar and the ceremony takes place beneath it.

Symbolic of the Orthodox ceremony is the Hebrew service, the benediction over the wine, the Aramaic pledge of fidelity and protection by the groom toward his bride, and the breaking of the ceremonial goblet.

In the Reform service, English as well as Hebrew is used in the ceremony, the canopy may be omitted, but many traditional elements may be preserved. The wedding procession, ceremony, and recessional function in the regular way. The bride and bridegroom usually drink out of the same cup, symbolizing the cup of joy.

The Home Wedding

A house wedding ceremony is exactly the same as a church ceremony. The procession, however, advances from the stairs down which the bridal party descends to an improvised altar. A marked-off enclosure may be set aside with chairs for the immediate family, or else they stand with the guests in the space provided. A prayer bench, or *prie dieu,* cushioned in white and decorated with flowers, is usually provided if the bride and groom are to kneel during the ceremony. Standards and ribbons, candelabra and kneeling bench are only necessary when they play a role in the ceremony. For most small home weddings, they are omitted.

At a house wedding the bride and groom do not take a single step together. The groom meets his bride at the point where the service is read, and after the ceremony, there is no recessional. When the clergyman withdraws, an usher removes the *prie dieu* and the bride and groom merely turn and receive the congratulations of their guests.

When there is no recessional, the groom always kisses the bride before they turn to receive their guests. At a church wedding, the groom does not kiss the bride at the altar, unless the clergyman is the bride's father or a relative who would ordinarily kiss her at the conclusion of the ceremony. In this case, the groom kisses her first. It is against all tradition for anyone to kiss the bride before her husband does.

At a house wedding, there are seldom more than four bridesmaids or four ushers, unless the house is enormously spacious and the wedding grandiose in scale.

A Marriage at the Parsonage, Clergyman's Study, or Judge's Chambers

For this type of wedding, the bride and bridegroom go together and are met there by members of their families and two or three invited friends. When all are gathered, the clergyman reads the service with the bride and bridegroom directly in front of him. At the end of the ceremony, the couple are congratulated by those present and then proceed to the place of reception.

Emily Post's Pointers to the Bride

When the rehearsal takes place, it is wise to have everyone understand his position in the receiving line.

On the wedding day, the bride wears her engagement ring on her right hand, and leaves her third finger left hand bare for the marriage ceremony. (Before the reception, she may slip her engagement ring over the wedding ring on her left hand.)

9

Modes and Manners for a Wedding Reception

ay, happy toasts, a dazzling bride's cake, a beaming bridal couple, and a few well-wishing friends are all it takes to make a perfect reception. In spirit, it is the occasion for the bride and groom to receive their wedding guests. In substance, it varies from the simplest fare to the most elaborate sit-down banquet, complete with orchestra. Both are perfect providing they are bright and sparkling and in keeping with the ceremony.

When there is no reception, it is customary for the bridal couple to receive the congratulations of their friends after the recessional, in the vestibule of the church. Otherwise, regardless of the type of reception or time of day, the receiving line proceeds in a definite order (see diagram on page 82).

The Receiving Line

Traditionally, the receiving line is composed of the bride and groom and the bride's attendants. *The ushers and best man never receive.*

As the hostess, the bride's mother (A) greets the guests near the door. The bride's father (B) may stand beside her, followed by the groom's mother (C) and father, or the fathers (F) may circulate among the guests. If it is more suitable to the room plan, the parents may also head the formal receiving line.

As the line forms, the bride stands on the bridegroom's right, the maid of honor at the right of the bride. Usually all the bridesmaids stand on the right of the maid of honor. At other times, half of them flank the maid of honor and the other half stand on the left of the bridegroom (if the parents do not take this position).

To all expressions of best wishes and congratulations, the bride and groom reply with a brief "Thank you." Long conversations are out of place and delay the progress of the receiving line.

Refreshments are usually served as soon as guests have passed through the receiving line.

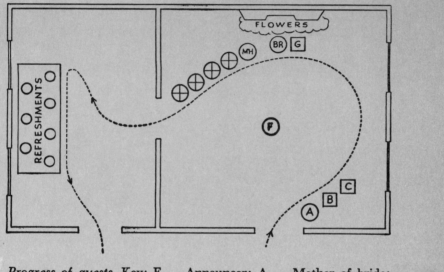

Progress of guests. Key: E — Announcer; A — Mother of bride; B — Mother of groom; C — Father of groom; F — Father of bride; G — Groom; Br — Bride; MH — Maid of honor; ⊕ — Bridesmaids.

The bride's father may receive if the bride has no mother. He may also ask a female relative to receive with him at the head of the receiving line.

Receiving the Guests

A warm, personal greeting to each guest is both gracious and proper. The bride always introduces her husband to those who have not yet met him, greets them by name, and thanks them for their wedding gift. The groom also introduces his friends and relatives to the bride, if she does not already know them.

The Sit-down Wedding Breakfast

The most elaborate wedding reception is the sit-down breakfast held at a hotel or club, or catered at the home of the bride. In addition to the floral decorations, embossed place cards are used on the bride's table and on the parents' table. Monogrammed menu cards, with cake boxes, matchbooks, and napkins to match may also be ordered as table appointments and gay souvenirs.

The caterer or banquet manager who handles the arrangements for your reception will charge you a fixed price per guest, depending on the menu you choose. In any case, the amount will cover silver, crystal, china, linens, tables, and chairs, if necessary, and service, too.

A typical menu for a sit-down breakfast would look like this:

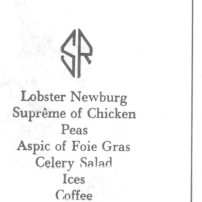

Lobster Newburg
Suprême of Chicken
Peas
Aspic of Foie Gras
Celery Salad
Ices
Coffee

For the most elaborate wedding breakfast, many delectable dishes, in varying courses may be served, but the only correct beverage is champagne.

The Bride's Table

The stunning highlight of the wedding breakfast is always the bride's table. At formal weddings, this table is decorated with white flowers and crowned with the elaborately tiered and iced wedding cake.

The bride sits at the right of the groom, the maid or matron of honor at his left. At the right of the bride is the best man, with ushers and bridesmaids seated alternately around the table. If some of the members of the bridal party are married, their mates are usually invited to sit at the bride's table. When there are no bridesmaids, the table is made up of intimate friends. Place cards are always used.

The Parents' Table

Unlike the other guest tables, the parents' table has place cards for those who have been invited to sit there. The groom's mother always sits on the right of the bride's father, and opposite them, the groom's father to the right of the

bride's mother. Other places are occupied by close friends, distinguished guests, and the clergyman and his wife.

The Toast to the Bride and Groom

At a sit-down bridal table, champagne is poured as soon as the first course is served. The bride's glass is filled first, then the bridegroom's glass, and then on around the table, ending with the best man seated at the right of the bride. At this time, anyone, although it is actually the duty of the best man, may propose a toast to the bride and groom. All, except the bridal couple, rise, raise their glasses, and drink the toast. Then the groom rises, expressing the thanks for both. Other toasts are usually proposed after the first one, to the bride's mother and others. The telegrams may then be read.

When there is no bride's table, the best man proposes the toast to the bride when the champagne is served.

At the end of the main course, the wedding cake is cut from the bottom tier by the bride and groom who share the first piece. The cake is then distributed to the guests by the caterer.

The Wedding Cake

The wedding cake, often called the bride's cake, is a "must" for every wedding reception, and should always look as pretty as a picture. Black fruit cake is traditional and most expensive, but light fruit cake and pound cake are equally popular.

While a caterer's cake is best and recommended for even the simplest reception, the fabulous wedding cakes pictured here are suggested to those brides with true confectioner's talents—or their mothers, or their cousins or their aunts!

Wedding Cake

(THREE OBLONG TIERS)

4 packages white cake mix
8 egg whites
5 cups water
2 teaspoons almond extract
  Lemon-Orange Wedding Cake Frosting

Empty contents of two packages of the mix into large bowl. Add 4 of the egg whites, 2½ cups of the water, and 1 teaspoon of the almond extract. Beat 3 minutes until smooth and creamy. Pour batter into two 13 x 9 x 2-inch pans, which have been greased and floured. Bake in moderate oven (350°F.) 30 to 35 minutes

Prepare the other two packages of cake mix as directed above. Pour batter into one 13 x 9 x 2-inch pan and one 9 x 9 x 2-inch pan, which have been greased and floured, dividing batter so as to have the same depth in each pan. Bake in moderate oven (350°F.) about 30 minutes for the 9-inch cake, 35 to 40 minutes for the 13 x 9 x 2-inch cake.

To Frost. Prepare Lemon-Orange Wedding Cake Frosting; reserve 2½ cups for decorating. Arrange two of the 13 x 9-inch layers, 13-inch sides together, on cardboard underliner on serving tray or board; then frost. Place remaining 13 x 9-inch cake

lengthwise on first tier and frost. For third tier, cut a 1-inch strip from opposite ends of the 9 x 9-inch layer to make a 9 x 7-inch layer. Place on second tier and frost.

To Decorate. With a cake decorator, use reserved frosting to make roses, leaves, floral garlands, or other desired decorations on cake top and sides. Top with wedding bell, flowers, or desired decoration.

Lemon-Orange Wedding Cake Frosting. (Mix this recipe twice to make enough frosting for three-tier wedding cake.) Measure 6 cups sifted confectioners' sugar. Cream ¾ cup shortening with ¼ teaspoon salt. Add part of the sugar gradually to creamed shortening, blending well after each addition. Then add remaining sugar, alternately with about ½ cup light cream until of right consistency to spread, beating after each addition until smooth. Add ½ teaspoon lemon extract and ½ teaspoon orange extract and blend.

Note: While frosting cakes, cover bowl with damp cloth to prevent hardening of frosting.

Wedding Cake

    3 packages white cake mix
3¾ cups water
    6 egg whites
1½ teaspoons almond extract
    Ornamental Frosting

Prepare each package white cake mix with 1¼ cups water and 2 egg whites as directed on package, adding ½ teaspoon almond extract to each batter. Grease and flour two 8-inch round pans and one 10-inch round pan. Spoon batters to equal depths in each pan. Bake in moderate oven (350°F.) for 30 to 40 minutes, or until done. Cool. Trim one 8-inch layer to make a 5-inch round layer. Frost cake with Ornamental Frosting, arranging layers as follows:

Place 10-inch cake on large flat tray or plate. Spread top and sides with thin layer of frosting. Center 5-inch layer on 8-inch cake. Frost. Then center upper layers on 10-inch base layer. Spread frosting over entire cake to give flat, even base for decorating. Place remaining frosting in cake decorating tube and decorate as desired. Garnish with silver dragees and flowers, if desired.

Ornamental Frosting

½ cup butter or margarine
½ teaspoon salt
  3 pounds (about 12 cups) sifted confectioners' sugar
  5 egg whites, unbeaten
¼ cup cream (about)
  2 teaspoons vanilla

Cream butter or margarine. Add salt and part of the sugar gradually, blending after each addition. Add remaining sugar, alternately with the egg whites first, then with the cream, until of right consistency to spread. Beat after each addition until smooth. Add vanilla; blend. (While frosting cake, keep bowl of frosting covered with a damp cloth to prevent drying.) Makes 5 cups of frosting.

Wedding Cake

3¾ cups sifted cake flour
4½ teaspoons double-acting baking powder
1½ teaspoons salt
2¼ cups sugar
  ¾ cups shortening (part butter)
1½ cups milk
1½ teaspoons vanilla
  3 eggs, unbeaten
    Cherry-Almond Filling
    Seven Minute Frosting

Measure sifted flour, add baking powder, salt, and sugar, and sift together. Stir shortening just to soften. Add dry ingredients, 1 cup milk, and the vanilla; mix well until all flour is dampened. *Beat 2 minutes* at a low speed of mixer or 300 vigorous strokes by hand. Add eggs and remaining milk and *beat 1 minute* longer.

Pour batter into three round 9-inch layer pans, which have been lined on bottoms with paper. Bake in moderate oven (375°F.) 20 to 25 minutes. Cool.

Prepare Cherry Almond Filling and spread between layers. Frost top and sides of cake generously with Seven Minute Frosting. Decorate top and base of cake with small fresh flowers.

Cherry Almond Filling. Combine 1 unbeaten egg white, ¾ cup sugar, dash of salt, ¼ cup of water, and 1½ teaspoons light corn syrup in top of double boiler. Beat 1 minute, or until thoroughly mixed. Then beat constantly over boiling water with sturdy egg beater (or at high speed of electric beater) 4 minutes, or until filling will stand in stiff peaks.

Remove from boiling water. For a very smooth and satiny filling, pour at once into a large bowl. Add ¾ teaspoon vanilla and beat 1 minute, or until thick enough to spread. Fold in ¾ cup chopped toasted blanched almonds, ¼ cup macaroon crumbs, 20 drained chopped maraschino cherries and, if desired, ¼ teaspoon lemon rind.

Festive Home Wedding Cake

     4 cups sifted cake flour
     5 teaspoons double-acting baking
       powder
 1½ teaspoons salt
     6 egg whites
   ½ cup sugar
     1 cup butter or shortening
     2 cups sugar
 1¾ cups milk
     2 teaspoons vanilla
       Wedding Cake Frosting and Fill-
       ing

Measure sifted flour, add baking powder and salt, and sift together three times. Beat egg whites until foamy, add ½ cup sugar gradually, and continue beating until meringue will hold up in soft peaks. Set aside.

Cream butter, add 2 cups sugar gradually, and cream together until light and fluffy. Add flour mixture, alternately with the milk, a small amount at a time, beating after each addition until smooth. Blend in vanilla. Then add meringue to cake batter and beat thoroughly into batter.

Pour batter into two 9 x 9 x 2-inch square pans, which have been lined on bottoms with paper. Bake in moderate oven (350°F.) 45 to 50 minutes.

To Frost: Cut each layer horizontally to make 4 layers in all. Prepare Wedding Cake Frosting and Filling. Place one layer on cardboard underliner which has been wrapped in waxed paper. Spread with one-third of the filling. Repeat with two other layers and rest of filling, topping with last layer. Swirl frosting attractively over top and sides of cake. Place cake on large tray and surround with greens or flowers, as desired.

Wedding Cake Frosting and Filling

3 egg whites, unbeaten
2¼ cups sugar
⅛ teaspoon salt
½ cup water
1 tablespoon light corn syrup
½ teaspoon grated lemon rind
1¼ cups finely chopped fruits and nuts*

Combine egg whites, sugar, salt, water, and corn syrup in top of a 2-quart double boiler. Beat about 1 minute, or until thoroughly mixed. Then place over boiling water and beat constantly with a sturdy egg beater (or at high speed of electric beater) 7 minutes, or until frosting will stand in stiff peaks. (Stir frosting up from bottom and sides of pan occasionally with rubber scraper, spatula, or spoon.)

Remove from boiling water. (For a smooth and satiny frosting, pour at once into a large bowl for final beating.) Add rind and beat 1 minute, or until thick enough to spread.

Fold fruits and nuts into about half of the frosting and use for the filling. Makes about 3½ cups filling and 3½ cups frosting.

* Suggested fruits and nuts are ¼ cup each finely chopped dates, white raisins, maraschino cherries, citron, and almonds.

The Stand-up Breakfast or Supper

The most typical collation for an afternoon or evening wedding is the buffet reception. If there is no bridal table, the wedding cake, flanked by floral pieces, is the prominent feature of the buffet table. At an elaborate high-noon breakfast, there are usually two or three cold dishes and at least two hot dishes.

The important thing is to select food that can be easily eaten with a fork while the plate is held in the other hand. Finger rolls and sandwiches should be substantial, yet small enough to eat daintily. Petits fours, mints, and ices or ice cream for dessert are also served. After-dinner coffee is served from a side table, as is the champagne or punch.

WEDDING RECEPTION BUFFET
Chilled Vichyssoise Soup
Tomato Aspic
Crab Meat Salad
Potato Chips
Wedding Cake
Coffee

Tomato Aspic

3 envelopes unflavored gelatin
1 cup cold water
4 cups tomato juice
1 teaspoon salt
4 peppercorns
1 bay leaf
2 stalks celery, chopped
¼ cup lemon juice
1 teaspoon onion juice
  crab meat salad
  Salad greens

Sprinkle gelatin on cold water to soften. Combine tomato juice, salt, peppercorns, bay leaf, and celery, in saucepan. Bring to boil and simmer 10 minutes. Strain. Add softened gelatin to hot liquid and stir until completely dissolved. Mix in lemon juice and onion juice. Pour into 12 (½ cup) heart-shaped molds. Chill until firm. Unmold onto serving plate. Spoon crab meat salad on top of each. Garnish with salad greens. Makes 12 servings.

Note: If heart-shaped molds are not available, pour mixture into 2 (9-inch) square pans. Chill, then cut with heart-shaped cutter.

Crab Meat Salad

½ pound cooked fresh crab meat
1 cup finely chopped celery
2 tablespoons finely chopped parsley
½ cup real mayonnaise

Clean and flake crab meat. Combine with remaining ingredients. Chill until serving time.

Note: 2 (5½- to 7½-ounce) cans crab meat may be used instead of fresh crab meat.

WEDDING RECEPTION BUFFET
Wedding Ring Salad
Party Chicken Salad
Hot Rolls
Strawberry Chiffon Pie
Wedding Cake
Coffee

Wedding Ring Salad

    2 (9-ounce) cans sliced pineapple
      Water
    5 envelopes unflavored gelatin
    2 (7-ounce) bottles lemon flavored
      carbonated beverage
  ¼ cup lemon juice
    1 (1 pound) can jellied cranberry
      sauce
    1 pound dry cottage cheese
  1½ cups chopped celery
    1 cup real mayonnaise
    1 teaspoon salt
      Salad greens

Drain pineapple; add water to liquid to
make 6 cups. Sprinkle gelatin on 1 cup liquid and let soften 5 minutes. Heat remaining liquid, but do not boil. Add softened
gelatin and stir until completely dissolved.

Mix in lemon-flavored beverage and lemon juice. Pour enough into 3-quart ring mold to form ½-inch layer. Chill until firm. Chill remaining gelatin to consistency of unbeaten egg white.

Cut pineapple slices in half and arrange on set gelatin layer in mold. Make 16 cranberry sauce balls, using melon ball cutter; place 1 in center of each half slice. Spoon enough of the chilling gelatin on top to cover. Chill until set. Fold cottage cheese, celery, mayonnaise, and salt into remaining gelatin. Spoon on top of set layers in mold. Chill until firm, 8 hours or overnight. Unmold onto serving plate. Garnish with salad greens. Makes 16 servings.

Party Chicken Salad

        8 cups large chunks of cooked
            chicken
        3 cups diced celery
      1½ cups real mayonnaise
        ⅓ cup lemon juice
        2 teaspoons salt
        ¼ teaspoon pepper
            Salad greens

Combine chicken and celery in large bowl. Stir lemon juice, salt, and pepper into mayonnaise, then pour over chicken and celery. Toss lightly, until well mixed. Arrange on salad greens. Serve with additional mayonnaise, if desired. Makes 16 servings.

Wedding Reception Punch

        3 ripe fresh peaches, unpeeled
        1 bottle (⅘) Sauterne
        1 teaspoon Angostura bitters
        2 bottles (⅘ each) Dry Champagne
            Fresh strawberries

Rub peaches well with damp cloth, then pierce deeply and thoroughly with tines of fork; place in bottom of punch bowl. Put ice block in punch bowl on peaches. Combine sauterne and bitters; pour into punch bowl and add champagne when ready to serve. Garnish punch and individual servings with fresh, unhulled strawberries. Makes about 25 servings.

The Simplest Reception

Mid-afternoon is the best time for the simple reception, when only the lightest

refreshments are necessary. A fruit or wine punch, to toast the bride and groom, and wedding cake are sufficient. More than this would include either tea or coffee, thin sandwiches, petits fours, nuts and mints.

Royal Champagne Punch

4 glasses (3¼-ounce each) bar-le-duc
2 cups Rosé
2 bottles Champagne
Large block of ice
Garnishes, to taste

Combine bar-le-duc and rosé. Chill several hours. Pour over ice in small punch bowl. Just before serving, add well-chilled champagne. Makes 20 to 25 punch cup servings. *Garnishes:* Feature a tray of choose-your-own garnishes near the punch bowl. Colorful suggestions are whole strawberries, sprigs of mint, lemon and lime slices, and such seasonal items as red currants, fresh cherries with stems.

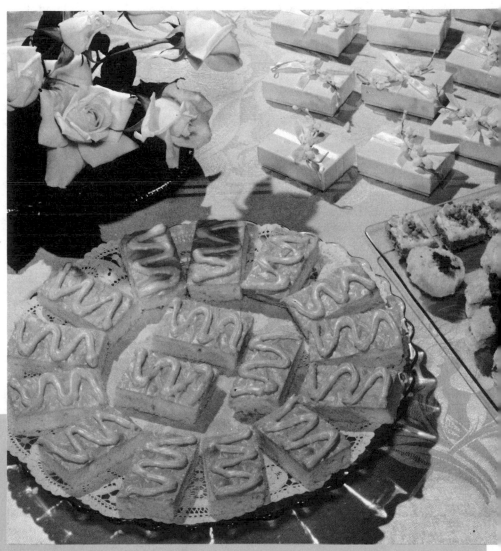

SIMPLE WEDDING RECEPTION
Assorted Sandwiches
Petits Fours
Assorted Nuts and Mints
Wedding Cake
Coffee

Assorted Sandwiches

CHEESE NUT SQUARES

1 (8-ounce) package cream cheese
3 tablespoons real mayonnaise
¼ cup chopped walnuts
10 slices whole wheat bread
   Chopped walnuts

Blend cream cheese with mayonnaise. Mix in ¼ cup chopped nuts. Trim crusts from bread, then cut each slice into 4 squares.

Spread with cream cheese mixture. Garnish with additional chopped nuts. Makes 40 squares.

SHRIMP PINWHEELS

½ pound cooked, peeled, cleaned shrimp
  Lemon juice
  Pepper
2 tablespoons real mayonnaise
1 loaf unsliced white bread
  Real mayonnaise
  Parsley sprigs

Chop shrimp very fine, then season with lemon juice and pepper. Stir in 2 tablespoons real mayonnaise and work to a paste. Trim crusts from bread and cut three lengthwise thin slices from loaf. Cut slices in half crosswise, then spread with additional mayonnaise and the shrimp mixture. Roll up each like jelly roll. Cover and chill until serving time. Cut each roll into 6 pinwheels. Serve garnished with parsley sprigs. Makes 3 dozen pinwheels.

Note: 1 (6½-ounce) can shrimp may be used instead of fresh shrimp.

Reserve remainder of loaf of bread for other tea sandwiches.

OLIVE MOONS

  White bread slices
¼ cup corn oil or balanced oil margarine
3 tablespoons finely chopped pimiento
  Stuffed green olives
  Pimiento strips

Cut 48 half-moon shapes from bread slices. Blend margarine with chopped olives. Spread on half the moon shapes, then top with remainder. Serve on platter garnished with pimiento strips. Makes 2 dozen.

Note: If half-moon cutter is not available, cut out with 1¾-inch circle cutter, then cut away ⅓ with same cutter to make ½ moons.

Note: All sandwiches should be wrapped in waxed paper, then in a damp cloth and chilled until serving time.

Petits Fours

3 cups sifted cake flour
1½ cups sugar
4 teaspoons baking powder
1 teaspoon salt
¾ cup corn oil margarine
¾ cup milk
4 egg whites
1½ teaspoons vanilla

Sift flour, sugar, baking powder, and salt together; reserve. Place margarine in mixing bowl; stir just enough to soften. Add sifted dry ingredients and ½ cup of the milk; beat 2 minutes at medium speed on electric mixer or 300 strokes by hand. Add egg whites, vanilla, and remaining ¼ cup milk; beat 1 minute with electric mixer or 150 strokes by hand. Pour into a greased and lightly floured 13 x 9½ x 2-inch rectangular cake pan. Bake in 375°F. (moderate) oven until tests done, 25 to 30 minutes. When cake is cool, cut into oblongs or squares and frost with Creamy Frosting.

Creamy Frosting

½ cup corn oil or balanced oil margarine
1 pound confectioners' sugar, sifted
1 egg
2 tablespoons water
  Food coloring

Cream margarine. Add half the confectioners' sugar, ½ cup at a time, beating until just smooth. Beat in egg. Add remaining confectioners' sugar, beating just until smooth and blended. Reserve 1 cup frosting; chill. Add water to remainder and beat until blended, then mix in desired coloring. Chill 30 minutes and spread on petits fours. Color reserved frosting as desired and use to decorate petits fours.

Hearts and Flowers Punch

- 2 bottles Rosé
- 2 cans frozen lemonade concentrate
  Heart-shaped ice mold
- 1 quart raspberry sherbet

Combine wine and lemonade concentrate; stir until concentrate melts. Pour over heart-shaped ice mold in small punch bowl. Put a spoonful of raspberry sherbet in each punch cup before ladling punch. Makes about 24 punch cup servings.

Note: If possible, chill wine before opening. *To make ice mold:* Fill aluminum-foil heart-shaped baking pan with water; freeze.

Music and Dancing

Any popular music played by an orchestra, ensemble, pianist, guitarist, or accordionist adds life and merriment to the party. If there is dancing, the bride takes the first dance with the groom, the second with her father-in-law, and third with her father. The groom follows the

same pattern. Then each dances with the bridesmaids, ushers, and other guests. The bride's father asks the groom's mother for the first dance and his father asks the bride's mother. The bride and groom usually continue dancing until the crowd begins to thin, or until the time when they must leave on their wedding trip.

The Throwing of the Bride's Bouquet

Before the bride changes into her traveling clothes, she usually ascends halfway up the stairs and throws her bouquet to the single bridesmaids and intimate girl friends gathered to catch it. It is a charming custom which decrees that the girl who catches it will be the next to be married. However, this eagerly anticipated ritual is sometimes omitted when a very close relative is too ill to attend the wedding, and the bouquet is sent to her.

Confetti and Rice . . . and They're Off!

After the couple has changed into going-away dress, and good-bys are said all around, the couple is usually whisked off in a flurry of confetti and rice by the members of the bridal party, close friends, and relatives. With them go the good wishes of all for a marriage filled with life's greatest rewards and pleasures!

Emily Post's Pointers to the Bride

A bride with cigarette is not a pretty picture. While you are wearing your wedding veil, remember not to smoke.

Don't forget to say good-by to your parents, attendants, and the groom's parents before you leave on your wedding trip.

A tense bride and temperamental groom detract from the serenity of the occasion. So remember to look happy and radiant on your wedding day!

10

A Postscript for the Wedding Guest

formal, engraved invitation to the church requires no answer whatsoever. However, if a reception card or invitation to the breakfast is included with an R.s.v.p., a reply is mandatory. The proper acceptance form, handwritten on the first page of a sheet of note paper, and following the spacing of the engraved style, reads:

Mr. and Mrs. Robert Gilding, Jr.
accept with pleasure
Mr. and Mrs. Smith's
kind invitation for
Tuesday, the first of June

The regret reads:

Mr. and Mrs. Richard Brown
regret that they are unable to accept
Mr. and Mrs. Smith's
kind invitation for
Tuesday, the first of June

Although the first names of the Smiths are omitted on the letter, they are included on the envelope, of course.

Replies to informal wedding invitations are also sent immediately and usually in the form in which they are received. Short, informal notes of reply are proper, although most answers to informal invitations are telephoned.

Combination Acceptance and Regret

It is entirely proper for a wife or husband to assume that either of them will be welcome alone at a reception. Therefore they send an acceptance worded as follows:

> Mrs. John Brown
> accepts with pleasure
> Mr. and Mrs. Smith's
> kind invitation for
> Saturday, the tenth of June
> but regrets that
> Mr. Brown
> will be absent at that time

The same wording sent by a husband would merely transpose Mr. and Mrs.

Sending the Wedding Present

While it is not obligatory, a wedding present is sent by most people who accept an invitation for the reception. Gifts are always sent from the store where they are purchased to the *bride,* even if the sender has never met her. Since the gift arrives in advance of the wedding, the bride's maiden name is used.

A wide range of wedding presents are suitable from silver, crystal, and china to linens; home furnishings, and housewares. The ideal gift is something useful or decorative for the home. A blank card or your own visiting card with "Best wishes" or "Best wishes for your happiness" should be enclosed with your gift. And if the bride does not already have your address, be sure to include it on the card.

Delayed presents. If, because of illness or absence, you cannot send the present until after the wedding, a note of explanation is proper. Delayed presents are always sent to Mr. and Mrs. Newlywed at their new address.

Presents for a second marriage are not expected, although a few close friends and relatives often wish to send a gift.

Checks as gifts. It is proper and customary for close relatives to present their gifts in the form of money. Checks

given as wedding presents are usually made out to the couple: Mr. and Mrs. John Newlywed, but they may be drawn to either the bride or groom.

Proper Dress for a Wedding

What you will wear to a wedding depends upon the size and time of the wedding and the custom of the community. Before noon women guests wear street-length daytime dresses. At noon and up to six P.M. skirts may be longer. Hats are required, gloves are correct, and flowers are never worn.

Even at big daytime weddings, men wear plain dark blue or gray suits. During hot weather, white or light gray flannel trousers with plain flannel coats are appropriate, but the sport coat is definitely out of place.

In certain cities in the South, tail coats are still required evening dress. At some formal weddings, tuxedos are worn in the evening. But in most communities, men wear plain, navy blue suits on all dress occasions for evening as well as daytime.

At a formal evening wedding, women wear evening gowns with scarves of lace or chiffon, or mantillas to cover their heads and shoulders for the church ceremony. At a simple wedding in the evening or during the day, afternoon dresses with small hats or veils are worn.

Guests who do not attend the reception wear whatever they usually wear to church. Children always wear their best party clothes.

At the Church

As a wedding guest, you are expected to arrive at least fifteen minutes before the ceremony. You will announce yourself as a "friend of the bride" or "friend of the groom" so that the usher may seat you on the left or right side of the church. If you have a reserved seat, present your card to the usher when you enter. No guest at a formal church wedding should seat himself.

Aisle seats need not be relinquished. If you arrive early enough to be given an aisle seat, it is entirely proper that you keep it, regardless of who or how many enter the pew later on.

Greeting other guests. It is entirely correct to greet the people you know in hushed tones, or by a smile or nod. If you find yourself seated among strangers, it is correct to sit quietly until the processional starts, when everyone rises. If you are in a church of a religious faith other than your own, it is correct to follow the example of the others. Stand if they stand, kneel when they kneel, sit when they sit, unless your religion forbids it. At an Orthodox or Conservative Jewish wedding, all men are expected to wear hats.

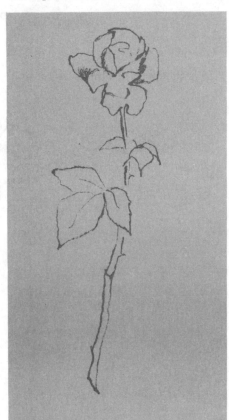

At the Reception

All guests are expected to provide their own transportation from the church to the reception. If you are an honored guest, one of the ushers will find transportation for you.

As you approach the receiving line, if there is no announcer, it is proper to take the hand of the bride's mother and announce your name to her. A short, sweet comment about the bride, or the wedding in general is tasteful. Most important, you always *congratulate the groom,* but you *wish the bride happiness.* It is a breach of etiquette to congratulate a bride on having secured a husband! If you are in doubt about whether the bride and groom know you, it is considerate to mention your name and wish them every happiness. Before leaving the reception, you should seek out the host and hostess, usually the parents of the bride, and thank them, as you would for any other occasion when you have been entertained.

The Congratulatory Telegram

Friends and relatives who are unable to attend the wedding may send a telegram to the couple, timed to arrive during the reception. Telegrams should always be addressed to the couple and never to the bride or groom alone. Any warm and friendly message is fitting, but the seriousness of the occasion should be respected. Attempts at humor are considered poor taste and are definitely out of place.

Emily Post's Point of Propriety

It is improper to bring children to a wedding unless they have been invited.

Your Wedding Memory Page

Name of Bride_____

Name of Groom_____

Wedding Date_____ Time of Ceremony_____

Place of Ceremony_____

Maid or Matron of Honor_____

Best Man_____

Bridesmaids_____   _____

_____   _____

_____   _____

Ushers_____   _____

_____   _____

Minister_____

Organist_____ Vocalist_____

Place of Reception_____

Number of Guests_____

Color Scheme of Wedding and Reception_____

Types of Flowers Used in Bridal Bouquets and Decorations_____

_____

Musical Selections Sung or Played at Ceremony _____

_____

Musical Selections Sung or Played at Reception _____

_____

Bride's Bouquet Caught By _____

"Something Old" _____, "Something New" _____

"Something Borrowed" _____, "Something Blue" _____

PRE-NUPTIAL SHOWERS AND PARTIES

Host or Hostess	Date	Number of Guests
_____	_____	_____
_____	_____	_____
_____	_____	_____
_____	_____	_____
_____	_____	_____
_____	_____	_____
_____	_____	_____
_____	_____	_____
_____	_____	_____
_____	_____	_____
_____	_____	_____

Gift Number	Present Received (Date)	MY WEDDING GIFT LIST			Where Bought	Thanks Written
		Article	Sent by	Sender's Address		

Picture Credits

Sketches by Irene McParland appear on pages 7, 12, 14, 17, 58, 65, 66, 67, 69, 70, 71, 75, 78, 84, 102, 103, 105, 107.

Page 2	Black, Starr and Frost
Page 3	Syracuse China Corp.
Page 4, top	The Taylor Wine Company, Inc.
Page 4, bottom	Black, Starr and Frost
Page 5	Best Foods Division, Corn Products Company
Page 20	Saks Fifth Avenue
Page 21	Saks Fifth Avenue
Page 23	Saks Fifth Avenue
Page 26	Vogue Pattern 4068, Vogue Pattern Service
Page 28	Vogue Pattern 148, Vogue Pattern Service
Page 30	Vogue Pattern 4185, Vogue Pattern Service
Page 31	Vogue Pattern 4185, Vogue Pattern Service
Page 32	Vogue Pattern 4244, Vogue Pattern Service
Page 33	Vogue Pattern 4244, Vogue Pattern Service
Page 34	Vogue Pattern 4218, Vogue Pattern Service
Page 35	Vogue Pattern 4218, Vogue Pattern Service
Page 36	Vogue Pattern 1091, Vogue Pattern Service
Page 38	Vogue Pattern 5413, Vogue Pattern Service
Page 39	Vogue Pattern 5413, Vogue Pattern Service
Page 41, left	Vogue Pattern 4252, Vogue Pattern Service
Page 41, right	Vogue Pattern 206, Vogue Pattern Service
Page 43	Syracuse China Corp.
Page 44	Best Foods Division, Corn Products Company
Page 45, top	Ocean Spray Cranberries, Inc.
Page 45, bottom	Franciscan Family China, Community Silverplate
Page 46	Best Foods Division, Corn Products Company
Page 47	The Taylor Wine Company, Inc.
Page 48, top	Franciscan Masterpiece China, Community Silverplate, Heirloom Community Silverplate
Page 48, bottom	Sunkist Growers
Page 49	Sunkist Growers
Page 50	Black, Starr and Frost
Page 51	The Gorham Company, the Belgian Linen Association
Page 52	Best Foods Division, Corn Products Company
Page 53	Best Foods Division, Corn Products Company
Page 54, top	Ocean Spray Cranberries, Inc.
Page 54, bottom	Best Foods Division, Corn Products Company
Page 55	Black, Starr and Frost
Page 58	Florists' Telegraph Delivery Association
Page 59	Florists' Telegraph Delivery Association
Page 60	Judith Garden, New York
Page 61	Judith Garden, New York
Page 62	Judith Garden, New York
Page 63	Judith Garden, New York
Page 64	Judith Garden, New York
Page 65	Columbia Records
Page 66	Columbia Records
Page 70	Plummer, McCutcheon, New York
Page 73	Plummer, McCutcheon, New York

Index